The Star Principle

A Faith-Based Approach
to Achieving Your Full Potential

PETER ADEBI

The Star Principle
by Peter Adebi

Printed in the United States of America

ISBN 1-59781-279-X

www.xulonpress.com

To my hearty little boys, Danny and Manny.

Table of Contents

❧

Introduction: The Star Principle..11

Section A. Self-discovery 17
- Chapter 1. Path to Your Destiny..............................19
- Chapter 2. The Making of a Star...............................35
- Chapter 3. Confronting Reality 43

Section B. Spiritual Development 67
- Chapter 4. Faith Premise...69
- Chapter 5. The Power of Thinking 79
- Chapter 6. The Power of Confession 89
- Chapter 7. Walking by Faith 99

Section C. Character Development...................................109
- Chapter 8. Unchanging Truth 111
- Chapter 9. Preparation 117

Section D. Resilience Development...................................127
- Chapter 10. Staying the Course 129
- Chapter 11. Overcoming Opposition 139
- Chapter 12. The Wisdom of Sharing 149

Section E. Self-leadership 159
- Chapter 13. Understanding Leadership 161
- Chapter 14. Faces of Leadership................................173
- Chapter 15. Readiness Assessment 193

"Remember your leaders, who spoke the word of God to you. Consider the outcome of their way of life and imitate their faith. Jesus Christ is the same yesterday and today and forever" (Hebrews 13:7-8 NIV).

Introduction

The Star Principle

Y ou hold in your hands the key to unlocking your full potential and becoming all that God has created you to be. You will learn how to recognize God's plan for your life and how to develop the leader in you so that you can achieve that plan.

The challenge of preparing for the future is one that none of us can escape. Without proper preparation, we can never experience our full potential. Although citadels of learning play a critical role in this preparatory process, they rarely offer programs that provide the spiritual and behavioral knowledge requisite for achieving the divine purpose for our lives. It is therefore not uncommon to find highly accomplished but deeply confused and miserable people. Even though they achieved something of significance, they are left with a void that their achievement cannot fill.

The struggle with this challenge is further evidenced in adolescents who make terrible life choices after high school, college students who spend years sampling several courses before resigning to one, job hoppers seeking an elusive fulfillment, steadily employed but perennially dissatisfied workers, and divorcees or couples considering a divorce. Although these examples are by no means exhaustive, they demonstrate the criticality of being adequately prepared to make the right decisions regarding one's future.

If you're among the people identified above, or if you've ever wondered about your destiny, about your future, or about what God has in mind for you, and if you've ever given some thought to how you might prepare yourself to achieve it, *The Star Principle* is for you.

To be clear, *The Star Principle* is not a doctrine about stars. It's not intended to advance the cause of astronomy, either. Instead, it explores the creationist and symbolic essence of stars in explaining God's purpose for every person.

The star represents the *ne plus ultra* of excellence. Above every other symbol, it typifies the success and fulfillment that every living soul should experience. It's so powerful a symbol that Jesus, our Lord, Savior, and model leader, called Himself the Bright and Morning Star (Revelation 22:16).

Christ desires for us to be like Him, and we have been equipped with all that we need to be just like Him. But in order to unleash your potential, you must first understand the principles by which He lived. This study closely examines the Bible to uncover these principles. It reviews several examples to demonstrate how they work. Some of the examples are reviewed multiple times to elucidate different aspects of their didactic qualities.

These principles are timeless and infallible. If you diligently apply them, you will achieve your full potential. They worked for the Old Testament followers of God. They worked for Christ and a majority of His disciples. They worked for the apostles and the early church. They will work for you too! Conversely, it's difficult for you to achieve your full potential if you're detached from the architect of your future.

Many leadership experts and inspirational or motivational speakers and writers have borrowed from these principles. However, they often water them down for reasons of political correctness and general acceptability. Thankfully, none of these constraints apply here. Your destiny is strictly yours to discover and it's too important to allow artificial barriers to get in the way.

A "principle" is a rule for putting together a predetermined pattern. The rule must be carefully adhered to or the product will deviate from the original. God has a blueprint of your future. He has provided principles that will enable you to create that design on earth. Your role is to discover and apply them.

These principles are not meant to operate in mutual exclusivity. They will not yield the desired result if applied piecemeal. When taken together, the principles that will enable you to achieve your full potential form a rule that I call *The Star Principle*. The thorough application of this rule results in resounding success.

The book is divided into five sections, each section focusing on one of the five aspects of *The Star Principle*. They include Self-discovery, Spiritual Development, Character Development, Resilience Development, and Self-leadership.

Self-leadership

The Star Principle

Resilience Development

Character Development

Self-discovery

Spiritual Development

Self-discovery. It's futile to attempt to discover what's in your future without first understanding who you are and from whence you came. This section is an exposition of how God sees you and how you should see yourself. It examines His will for you and discusses primary steps toward achieving it.

Additionally, it tackles such complex topics as destiny, potential, sin, life, and death. It exposes inherent weaknesses that can prevent you from achieving your full potential and provides guidance on how to overcome them. At the end of the section, you should have a preliminary understanding of God's purpose for your life, how to access supernatural enablement to achieve that purpose, and how to overcome personal weaknesses.

Spiritual Development. It's one thing to know and believe that God exists; it's quite another to maintain a relationship with Him. This section begins by probing the concept of faith. It goes on to analyze faith's role in preparing for a divinely appointed future. Specifically, it examines the power of thinking and confession in accessing divine provisions.

You will discover where and how thoughts originate, how they are related to your destiny, and how, through your confessions, you can translate them into action. You will also learn how imperative it is to walk by faith. Ultimately, this section will cast light on your spiritual life and its role in enabling you to experience your full potential.

Character Development. Any faith-based approach requires certain irreducible standards of behavior. These standards are to be ingrained in a person's character. But character building is not the forte of most educational systems. Ironically, it is often the bane of many an accomplished person. The number of industry captains in US jails is a case in point. These leaders never planned to spend their retirement in a penitentiary. More than likely, a character flaw—greed, lust, dishonesty, etc.—landed them there.

Although a number of other sections also touch on character building, this one sheds light on the core of the immutable character of God. Truth originates from Him, and justice and equity are derived from it. Those who look to Him for direction must learn to uphold and defend truth. The unjust must understand that they will inevitably receive the same justice they mete out to others.

The section closes by discussing the essence of self-discipline in preparing for the future. It builds on the central thrust of the book, which is that adequate and proper preparation is the *sine qua non* of achieving your full potential.

Resilience Development. Perhaps you've seen people who started out well but somewhere in their journey, something happened—they lost focus, forgot where their help comes from, surrendered to opposition, etc. As a result, they gave up on their dream.

God didn't intend for you to abandon your future. You must take the necessary steps to dust off that rusty vision and continue where you left off. This section shows you how.

Leadership development. The book closes with an overview of the origin, meaning, and dimensions of leadership. It presents leadership as the orchestra conductor that harnesses and organizes the other aspects of *The Star Principle* to achieve the desired result.

You must apply leadership principles and skills in yourself first before attempting to lead others. A person who is unable to lead himself is not worthy to lead others.

Lastly, this book includes a self-assessment that will enable you to ascertain your readiness to take on the future and attain all that is intended for you. It is my sincere hope that by the time you get to this section, you will have discovered the truth about your future and the process for bringing it to pass.

To get the most benefit out of this book, I encourage you to have a pencil and notepad in hand as you study it. The point is not how quickly you can complete it but what you gain from it. Make note of the points that leap off the page into your heart and apply them to your life. After you've read the book once, revisit it as often as necessary until it's ingrained in your value system and daily living.

This book is based on God's Word, and He promises that His word will not return to Him void; it must accomplish what it was sent to do (Isaiah 55:11). Therefore, if you believe, it will change your life for the best!

Self-discovery

CHAPTER 1

Path to Your Destiny

Topics such as self-discovery, destiny, the right path to the future, and life after death lend themselves to extensive, convoluted, and contentious philosophical discourse. Sages of all generations have wrestled with them, but they often generate more questions than answers. Yet more people than ever are joining the quest.

What's at the bottom of the overwhelming interest in these subjects? The simple answer is that humanity is in search of the truth. We yearn to know who we are and how we got here. We focus on developing our abilities so we can better explore the world, the essence of the exploration being to discover the truth about our earthly existence.

The intent here is not to elongate the philosophical conundrum. Rather than investigate myriad perspectives, we will focus on a potent, timeless, and proof-laden source that holds the truth about humankind and our purpose on earth. It's the authoritative source for human spirituality. No other voice speaks as boldly about the topics at issue. This source is the inexorable Word of God, the Bible, written by over forty authors under the inspiration of the Holy Spirit.

Also known as the Word, the Scriptures, or the Holy Book, the Bible is unequivocal in stating that humanity is not here by happenstance. *We were each created for a purpose, and there is a clear and dependable path to achieving that purpose.* The Bible provides a roadmap that includes all the warning signs and troubleshooting tips we will ever need. However, it is our responsibility to become adept at using the map on our journey.

The capability to correctly, consistently, and effectively utilize the map is called leadership. To better understand leadership, however, we must discover more about ourselves.

We were created by God.

Genesis 1:26 states that God created man in His "image" and "likeness." The word *image* indicates that man has a physical resemblance to his Maker.

Likeness suggests similitude in personality or mannerism. God put a piece of His divine nature in man. He breathed His spirit into him so that man, like Him, would live eternally (Genesis 2:7). He further equipped man with the mind and intelligence to be able to relate to Him. He created Adam as a son, a friend.

God put Adam in the middle of the garden of Eden, an inimitable landscape of winding rivers, luscious greenery, and friendly animals. However, He knew that it wouldn't be long before Adam got bored with tending the plants and animals. He needed a peer, a companion. God also wanted him to reproduce and fill the earth (Genesis 1:28). He therefore put Adam to sleep and performed the first and last surgery of its kind. Taking one of Adam's ribs, He made a woman from it.

God could have created the woman as He created Adam. Instead, He laid the foundation for the unity of body and spirit in a marital relationship. That's why Genesis 1:24 states that a man and his wife are one flesh. All of humanity originated from this first marriage.

Purpose: What are we here for?

At creation, God gave the first humans authority over the creatures in the sea, the birds in the air, and all the living things on the ground (Genesis 1:26). He empowered them to manage the garden and to eat of the produce except for the fruits from a particular tree (Genesis 2:17).

God's unmistakable purpose is that humans do His will on earth. Jesus demonstrated this truth on several occasions. When He was interrupted with a message that His mother and siblings were looking for Him, His response was that whoever does God's will is His brother and sister and mother (Mark 3:35). He taught His disciples to pray that God's will would be done on earth as it is in heaven (Matthew 6:10). Upon realizing in Gethsemane the enormous suffering that faced Him, He wept before God and asked if the suffering could be removed. However, He qualified the request by asking that the will of God be done (Mark 14:36).

As long as they lived in obedience to God's will, Adam and Eve were God's ambassadors in the earth and would continue to build on the good work that He had established.

No substitute for obedience. God requires unconditional obedience from us. When He imparted Himself into man, He implanted the *ability to choose.* Since He represents everything good, He requires the only creature modeled after Him to willfully acknowledge His goodness and lordship and therefore obey Him. This is of extreme importance because obedience is the highest form of worship we can give Him. Isaiah 43:7 proclaims that He created everything for His glory, and His glory He will share with no one (Isaiah 43:7; 42:8). Although He has the power to force obedience, doing so would have placed humans no higher than the animals and made Him a liar.

Deuteronomy 11:27 adds that obedience will bring us blessings, and God reinforced that promise through the prophet Isaiah: "If you are willing and obedient, you shall eat the good of the land" (Isaiah 1:19). Indeed, God's will for our lives is wrapped in our obedience. All the blessings and promises in the Scriptures are tied to it. The lives of the people we will examine throughout this book were shaped by their positions on total obedience to God. Our future depends on it.

God's will. If obedience to God's will is of such great significance, it behooves us to examine what His will contains. *Goodness* is our first insight into God's will. God is good and is the source of all good. James 1:17 confirms that every good and perfect gift comes from Him. Psalm 31:19 exalts His goodness. Psalm 33:5

acknowledges that the earth is full of His goodness. On the sixth day of creation, He surveyed His handiwork and "it was very good" (Genesis 1:31). Paul affirms in his letter to Timothy that "every creature of God is good" (1 Timothy 4:4). Indeed, the entire Bible is a eulogy to God's goodness.

God's expectation is that human beings will operate in goodness. Our trailblazer, Jesus, operated in goodness throughout His ministry (Acts 10:38). Ephesians 2:10 declares that "we are God's workmanship, created in Christ Jesus to do good works" (NIV). We are to hold on to what is good (1 Thessalonians 5:21), follow what is good (1 Thessalonians 5:15), be zealous to do good (Titus 2:14), thrive in doing good work (2 Corinthians 9:8), and be productive in every good work (Colossians 1:10). We are to diligently assess everything we engage in to ensure that it represents the good, acceptable, and perfect will of God for us (Romans 12:2). And raising the instructions to a higher level, James notes that it is sinful to avoid doing good (James 4:17).

Understanding what *good* means from God's perspective is a germane step in your journey toward achieving your full potential. From researching the Hebrew and Greek origins of the word as used in the Bible, three forms of goodness become apparent. They include (1) virtuousness; (2) mercy, kindness, and favor; and (3) work that produces benefit.

The Greek root *kalos* means "virtuous" or "worthy." It refers to God's holy nature. Isaiah's prophetic ministry began with a vision of God's holiness (Isaiah 1:1-4). He lamented his impure state once he realized how holy God is (vs. 5). God requires us to be holy (1 Thessalonians 4:7). We can neither maintain a relationship with Him nor see Him someday without holiness (Hebrews 12:14). Prior to Adam and Eve disobeying Him in the garden, they were holy. That means they were pure or without sin in His presence. However, once they listened to Satan and exercised their will against God, they lost their relationship with Him. For us to operate in goodness as God requires, we must be holy.

By making the wrong choice, the first couple brought judgment upon themselves and their posterity. Pain, suffering, difficulty, enmity, violence, disease, and death resulted from their disobedience (Genesis 3:14-21). Judgment was executed on the basis of another character of God, which is righteousness. It made no difference who they were or what connection they had to Him. God doesn't condone sin in anyone. He does what is right in every situation. Satan (aliases: Lucifer, fallen angel, devil, accuser, thief, liar) was a high-ranking angel in heaven before he thought about contending for God's throne. In consequence, God immediately executed justice, cast him out of heaven, and sentenced him to eternal damnation (Isaiah 14:12-15).

No matter how moral Adam and Eve tried to be after their separation from God, their best efforts would never have been sufficient to reverse the curse they brought on themselves and restore their relationship with God. The same is true of us today. Some people believe that living by a secular code of ethics makes them worthy and acceptable before God. Nothing could be further from the truth! The Bible states that our righteousness is like filthy rags before God (Isaiah 64:6). God's righteousness that was on Adam and Eve was compromised when they disobeyed Him. They passed down their sin and the consequent punishment to all humankind (Romans 5:12). The only way to restore the relationship that was lost in the garden is through faith in Jesus Christ.

Mercy, kindness, and favor represent another form of goodness. This form traces its origin to the Hebrew word *checed.*

God's mercy is unrivaled. Several Scriptures note that His mercy endures forever (1 Chronicles 16:34, 41; 2 Chronicles 5:13; 7:3, 6; Ezra 3:11; Psalm 106:1; 107:1; 118:1; 136:1; Jeremiah 33:11). Jeremiah adds that His mercies are new every morning (Lamentations 3:23).

Despite the moral bankruptcy of our world, we are not consumed because of His mercies (Lamentation 3:22). Regardless of who we are, where we've been, or what we've done, if we turn to God with a repentant heart, we will find mercy. He expects us to do the same for our fellow human beings (Proverbs 3:3; 14:3; Micah 6:8).

God's character is also marked by everlasting kindness (Isaiah 54:8). Kindness is His capacity to do the right thing for us when we don't expect or deserve it. It's also His tendency to exceed our expectations. Adam didn't ask for a companion before God perceived the need and made one (Genesis 2:18). Sarah, Abraham's wife, was barren when God called them. They would have been pleased with just one child. Instead, God birthed an entire nation through them (Genesis 12:2). Solomon asked only for an understanding heart. He received it, along with untold honor and riches (1 Kings 3:3-13).

Jesus stated, in Luke 6:35, that He is kind even to unthankful and evil people. He sends rain on the just and the unjust (Matthew 5:45). Paul wrote that God "is able to do exceedingly abundantly above all that we ask or think" (Ephesians 3:20). With God on our side, there will be no end to pleasant surprises. The goal is to allow His kindness to radiate through us.

Favor is a mark that God puts on His children so they will prosper in all that they do. It converts the machinations of the enemy into a springboard for success. When divine favor is on you, every event in your life must align with your God-given future.

Joseph had a couple of great dreams in which he saw himself exalted above everyone in his family. His brothers already hated him for being their father's favorite, and the dreams made matters worse. Some of them wanted him dead, but God's favor was working in his behalf. Reuben and Judah intervened. Instead of allowing him to be killed, they sold him into slavery. In one of his difficult experiences as a slave, Joseph was wrongfully imprisoned. There, the Bible records, because of divine favor, the prison guard treated him kindly. Ultimately, that favor caused him to interpret the dreams that opened the door to Pharaoh's court. He subsequently became Pharaoh's second in command. Upon reuniting with his brothers, Joseph made a statement that underscores the power of divine favor: What the enemy meant for evil, God meant for good (Genesis 37:1-36; 39:21; 40:1-23; 41:1-45; 50:20).

Similarly, when the people of Israel were preparing to leave Egypt, God gave them favor with the Egyptians. The Egyptians had suffered severe plagues that culminated in the deaths of their first-born sons. They knew the Israelites were leaving for good. Yet when the Israelites asked to borrow their gold and silver jewelry, their response couldn't have been more munificent (Exodus 3:21; 12:35-36).

Everything in your path kowtows to your future when God is

leading the way. As Paul put it, "If God is for us, who can be against us?" (Romans 8:31). The Bible states that "*all things* work together for good to those who love God" (emphasis mine) and have been called according to His purpose (Romans 8:28). The only way you can join the ranks of the called is if you respond. If you haven't responded, Christ is calling today; don't ignore His voice.

Favor is a godly attribute that we must emulate. Indeed, an integral part of walking in obedience is showing favor to others (Psalm 112:5). Though we're not omnipotent, if we determine in our hearts to be active and instrumental in enabling others to succeed, God will use us accordingly. Your acts of favor will never go unrewarded (Matthew 10:46).

The third form of goodness is *agathos.* That's a Greek word that means "good work" or "work that produces benefit." God is the authority at doing good work. Heaven and earth, the moon and stars, winter and summer, night and day, rain and snow, plants and animals, and, of course, all of humanity are irrefutable evidence of His hard work. The depth and ingenuity of His work are incomparable. The entire universe owes its stability to His flawless design. Though He created billions of entities, He effectively oversees all of them.

God requires us to be actively engaged in doing good work. We should seek opportunities to work, and we should take every job seriously (Titus 2:14; Colossians 1:10). We must eschew eye service and ensure that all our work is acceptable to Him (Matthew 23:5; Ecclesiastics 12:14). God is not enthused by couch potatoes. The Bible instructs us to do good work with our hands (Ephesians 4:28; 1 Thessalonians 4:11). It warns that laziness soon leads to poverty (Proverbs 6:10-11). It adds that those who are too lazy to work should be kept away from food (2 Thessalonians 3:10).

You must understand God's position on the work (occupation, vocation) you do, as your destiny is tied to it. Ephesians 2:10 tells us that He's interested in the work we do: "For we are God's workmanship, created in Christ Jesus to do good works, which *God prepared in advance for us to do*" (NIV, emphasis mine). Not only is He interested in what you do, He predetermined the work you should do. There are no coincidences when you walk with Him.

Every work you do is an unfolding of your future.

That said, one key question remains unanswered: How can you be certain that the work you do or desire to do is what God intends for you? Did He intend for you to be a writer, teacher, preacher, painter, or physician? The answer is found in the following Scripture: "It is God who works in you to *will* and to *act* according to His good purpose" (Philippians 2:13 NIV, emphasis mine). If you're a believer, God puts thoughts in your heart and enables you to translate those thoughts into action. The actions that result from your thoughts constitute your destiny. This fact underscores the danger in ignoring, despising, or undermining the sparks of ideas and occasional "eureka moments" that you experience. They are divinely imparted to actualize God's plan for your life.

Throughout this work, I will refer to God's purpose for our lives as *God-given future, intended future, desired future,* or *destiny.* When God transmits His purpose for your life to your heart, it becomes yours: your desire, your passion, your dream, your vision. The appropriate next step is to thankfully acknowledge who it came from, document and refine it, and seek guidance in bringing it to fruition.

Talent: Do I have what it takes?

God has imbued every human being with a talent or gift. A talent is a unique ability that enables a person to excel in a field of endeavor and, ultimately, achieve his or her destiny. Abraham was an extraordinary man of faith; Joseph, an excellent interpreter of dreams; Joshua, a gifted military strategist; David, a talented singer and poet; Solomon, an incredibly wise leader. Talent enabled them to reach the pinnacle of their destinies. Your gift will make a way for you and cause you to reach an exalted position (Proverbs 18:16).

In order for your gift to work for you, you have to discover and polish it. A surefire path to discovery is giving your best effort to every opportunity that comes your way. As Solomon put it, "Sow your seed in the morning, and at evening let not your hands be idle, for you do not know which will succeed, whether this or that, or whether both will do equally well" (Ecclesiastes 11:6 NIV).

If a seed doesn't succeed, that doesn't necessarily imply that you've sidestepped your destiny. God uses all of our experiences to prepare us for the future. Moses was a prince in Egypt before anger got the best of him and he fled into exile. In a matter of days, he went from being an heir to the throne of Pharaoh to a desert dweller. He ended up a shepherd in the desert for forty years. Most people would have agreed that his career was over. He'd had his chance and blew it. But God had a different intention. He had plans for Moses to lead His people out of slavery. However, He needed to put Moses through an anger management course first. After the course, Moses earned a reputation as the meekest man on earth. He was subsequently able to lead the Israelites out of Egypt (Exodus 2:1-25; 4:18-31; 14:1-31).

It's ungodly to ignore your talent. Jesus illustrated this point in the parable of the talents. In this story, a man traveling to a distant country gave each of his three servants talents to invest. He gave them five talents, three talents, and one talent, respectively.

The servant who received five talents invested it and doubled his principal. The servant who received two talents did likewise and also made 100 percent on his investment. But the servant who received one talent buried it in the ground. He was angry at his master, just as some people are angry at their Creator today.

When the master returned, he was pleased with the two profitable servants and consequently promoted them into leadership positions. The ungrateful servant was fired, and his talent was taken away and given to the servant who had the most talents (Matthew 25:14-30).

To begrudge or compare one's talent to that of others is to accelerate the future in the wrong direction. No matter how inconsequential you think your talent is, you have a duty to invest it wisely. That's what God expects, and that's what will bring you success.

Potential: How much can I accomplish?

How big is God? Consider the harmonic tapestries of flora and fauna, corralled by a web of oceans and lakes, interlaced with beads of precious stones and minerals, laid out to benefit humanity. They are but a drop in the bucket among all of God's creation (Isaiah 40:15). The Bible notes that heaven is His throne and the earth His footstool (Isaiah 66:1). Yet, as incomprehensively vast as the universe may be, He governs everything and everyone He has created, and nothing happens without His knowledge.

What's more, the only resource that was needed at creation was His word. He makes things out of nothing by calling things that don't exist into being as though they existed. "Let there be light," He commanded, and instantly, there was light. He made a dry path through the Red Sea, caused water to flow from a rock, and confounded Israel's enemies (Genesis 1:3; Exodus 14:21; Numbers 20:11; Exodus 14:14). He is the God of infinite possibilities.

How big are your dreams? Do you know that the One who has called you is able to fulfill His purpose for your life? With God on your side, your potential is unlimited. If you can dream it, you can achieve it. Paul wrote that we can "do all things through Christ" who strengthens us (Philippians 4:13). Christ added that with God all things are possible (Matthew 19:26). If you ask anything of Him in Christ's name, as long as you're living in obedience, it shall be done (John 14:13). This is one of the reasons a healthy relationship with Him is indispensable. Not only will you receive visions about your future, He will provide step-by-step guidance until every last bit of it is achieved. The Scriptures substantiate this point by stating that God, who has begun a good work in you, is able to complete it (Philippians 1:6).

Paul had divine guidance and was therefore able to declare victory at the end of his ministry. "I have fought the good fight, I have finished the race, I have kept the faith" (2 Timothy 4:7). We can do the same if we walk closely with God.

Your potential is not a factor of your personal or environmental condition. Moses was born to slave parents and abandoned as a baby on the side of a river. He was born at a time when all Hebrew male children were being killed at birth, and his mother was hoping he would fall into safe hands. Moses' prospect for survival was slim to none. Yet of all his peers, he received the most privileged upbringing. God had determined his path, and not even Pharaoh could have stopped him.

As a senior political leader in Egypt, Moses nurtured a dream about liberating his people from their oppressors. He failed at his first attempt and consequently fled into the desert. While in exile, he met Zipporah, landed a job with her family, married her, and had a son. He became so comfortable in his new environment that his dream began to slip away. Better to be content with a family who supported him than to undertake the risk of challenging Pharaoh to free Israel. How often we settle for mediocrity and allow our dreams to fritter away in the face of opposition.

Moses gave every excuse he could muster to keep from fulfilling his destiny. He was keenly aware of his limitations, including a speech impediment. He believed he lacked the potential to accomplish the job. He was right. Destiny is not about what we can accomplish on our own. It's about what God has purposed to accomplish through us. The Bible says that on our own we can do nothing (John 15:5).

God, who had put the desire in Moses' heart and had witnessed his initial passion and effort, was willing to nudge him along. In His mercy, He took the time to speak with him about the need to return to Egypt. He promised to be with him and to deliver Israel from the hands of Pharaoh (Exodus 2:1-25; 3:1-22; 4:1-31). Moses' faith was strengthened and he embarked on the journey. He subsequently achieved his dream.

Never underestimate the importance of spending time with God. There is no knowing what would have happened had Moses fled from the presence of God. If you haven't done so already, develop a habit of communicating with God daily through praise, prayer, and studying the Word. Allow Him to speak to you by meditating on the Word. He will equip you with the right response to every situation (Exodus 13:1-22; 14:1-31).

It's a fallacy to think that your knowledge, skills, and abilities are ultimately responsible for your success. The Word bears out this fact in Ecclesiastes 9:11 (NIV): "The race is not to the swift or the battle to the strong, nor does food come to the wise or wealth to the brilliant or favor to the learned; but time and chance happen to them all." *Time* in this Scripture refers to God's schedule for your life. The fact that your dream hasn't materialized five years after you had it isn't necessarily an indication of a problem or failure. Abraham and Sarah had to wait on God's time to have Isaac.

Although Hannah was faithful in serving God, she went childless for several years. Her mate's mockery caused her anguish, but that didn't open her womb any sooner. At the appointed time, God answered her prayers and she bore a child, who became the mighty prophet Samuel (1 Samuel 1:1-28).

When God says it's time for your dream to come to fruition, no external force, mortal or immortal, can stop it. Once more, Joseph's story comes to mind. By selling him into slavery, his brothers thought they would obliterate his dream. As a prisoner, his primary concern would have been to breathe the air of freedom again. But from God's perspective, it was time for him to rise to national leadership in Egypt. Joseph's circumstance at that moment made no difference.

John wrote that when the Lord opens a door, no one can shut it, and when He shuts it, no one can open it (Revelation 3:7). The issue for Christians is not whether God has opened a door to their desired future. There is always an open door before us. The challenge is in walking closely, patiently, and faithfully with God to be able to go through it. The only one who can truncate your intended future is you! We do this by the choices we make whether to obey God or not. God's thoughts toward us are always for good, not evil (Jeremiah 29:11). But we have to demonstrate through obedience that we agree with Him. The Bible says that before us are life and death, curses and blessings. It counsels us to choose life so that God's plan for our lives may be fulfilled (Deuteronomy 30:19).

Adam and Eve lost their intended future when they ate the forbidden fruit. Cain brought a curse on his future by murdering his brother Abel (Genesis 4:8). Their choices brought condemnation to their lives. In light of their mistakes, consider this: What are your choices bringing into your life?

With God, elective obedience is unacceptable. We cannot obey God only when it's convenient. A single act of disobedience can cost us eternity with Christ. No one knows this better than Moses. He had been diligent in obeying God until he was instructed to speak to a rock so the rock would produce water. Instead, he struck the rock twice. That act of impetuousness cost him entry into the Promised Land (Numbers 20:8-12).

In Ecclesiastics 9:11, the term *chance* in the last phrase means "opportunity." Sometimes people blame a less-than-desirable lot in life on a lack of opportunity. Difficult childhood experiences, financial hardship, and physical disability are some of many perceived inhibitors to being able to compete on a level playing field with others. But no person, thing, or circumstance can deprive you of your destiny. If you put forth your best effort at every opportunity that comes your way, God will lead you to your breakthrough. Had Joseph refused to put his talent to use by not interpreting the dreams of his fellow inmates, he would have missed the opportunity to meet Pharaoh.

Naaman, general of the army of Syria, needed to be cured of leprosy. He was looking forward to the opportunity to meet Elisha, a prophet of God, to get healed. While he was waiting in front of Elisha's house, the prophet sent a messenger to instruct him to go bathe seven times in the Jordan River. Infuriated that Elisha didn't take the time to meet him personally and perform a healing act, he stormed out of his compound with no intention of bathing in the Jordan. However, one of his servants intervened by encouraging him to obey the prophet, and he listened. Never let pride dictate the opportunities you take. Pride is of the devil and the Bible says that it's the forerunner of destruction (Proverbs 16:18). Naaman's leprosy disappeared after the seventh bath in the Jordan (2 Kings 5:1-14). Had he ignored the word of the prophet because it fell short of his expectation, he probably would have died leprous.

Life, success, sin, and death.

The biggest constraint to achieving your God-given future is the sin chromosome. Humanity inherited the sin nature from Adam (Romans 5:12; 3:23). It eventually leads to destruction and death (Romans 6:23).

The only escape from the curse of sin is the transformation that occurs when you accept Christ as your personal Lord and Savior (2 Corinthians 5:17). Christ came that you may have abundant life (John 10:10). The plan that God has for you consists in the life that Christ spoke of.

One of the worst mistakes we can make is to interpret earthly success as sign of a wholesome relationship with God. Success is not measured by the status or wealth you've achieved, but by the degree to which your achievements align with the will of God for your life.

The Bible states that there is a way that seems right to us, but the end of it is death (Proverbs 16:25). The devil is adept at offering counterfeit success. To tempt Jesus, he took Him up on a particularly high mountain, from which He could see the kingdoms of the world and their glory. He promised to give Jesus everything He saw if He would only worship him (Matthew 4:1-11).

After more than two thousand years, enticement remains a potent weapon in the devil's arsenal. Jesus was able to overcome because He knew that every good and perfect gift comes from God. He understood Proverbs 10:22: "The blessing of the Lord brings wealth, and He adds no trouble to it" (NIV). The devil has no free gift. His gifts are not perfect. What he offers is contrived and fleeting bliss that's a perversion of your future. Give him and his gifts no place in your life.

God's original plan was for humanity to live and reign eternally with Him. Adam, through disobedience, undermined that plan, but God restored it through Jesus Christ. (See Romans 5:12-21.) Those who accept Jesus will experience great success on earth. However, success in a sinful world cannot be compared to what God offered the first couple in the garden. Pain, suffering, disease, and death were not in the mix.

Even with all its glorious splendor, the garden doesn't compare to the eternity that awaits overcomers. If the devil meant to rob humanity of the garden, he must have been horrified when God opened up His kingdom for us. The Scriptures reveal in 2 Timothy 2:12, Revelation 3:21, and Revelation 20:6 that overcomers—that is, those who keep the will of the Father on earth—will reign with Christ in the kingdom of God.

Looking beyond the grave at the close of his ministry, Paul declared that a crown of righteousness awaited him (2 Timothy 4:8). This is what makes the Christian life incomparable. You triumph in this life by divine enablement and receive a crown for your effort in the life after. This is the future that I desire. How about you?

What next?

God has a purpose for you and it is good! He's made provisions for you to achieve it. Second Timothy 3:16-17 enunciates the pivotal role of the Word in helping you to attain all He has planned for you: "All Scripture is given by inspiration of God, and is profitable for doctrine, for reproof, for correction, for instruction in righteousness, that the man of God may be complete, thoroughly equipped for every good work." Your responsibility is to understand and tap into His provisions for the purpose to materialize in your life. We will continue the discovery by taking a closer look at who you are.

CHAPTER 2

The Making of a Star

People are often mesmerized by the majestic presence of a shining star. These awesome heavenly bodies have been around from creation and continue to inspire countless scholastic research. You don't have to be an astronomer to understand why humankind is so captivated by this celestial gem.

As you ponder the remainder of this chapter, it will dawn on you that we have more in common with stars than you've probably ever imagined.

In reviewing the Bible, I found the word *star* or *stars* more than sixty times. It struck me that there must be something significant about the star for it to have appeared so many times. Each appearance of the word reinforced the fact that, just like everything else that was created, stars were made for a purpose.

Stars provide direction. Genesis 1:14-19 states that God made the stars "for signs and for seasons," and to "give light on the earth." Jeremiah 31:35 reinforces that "God gives the stars for a light by night."

The story of the Magi (three wise men) who came from the east to visit Jesus at birth comes to mind. These men saw a star that was a sign of Jesus' birth, and following the guidance of the star, they were able to locate Him (Matthew 2:9). During His ministry on earth,

Jesus declared to His disciples, "I am the way, the truth, and the life. No one comes to the Father except through Me (John 14:6)." Just as the star led those wise men to the Messiah, Jesus leads us to the Father. Likewise, He has called us to lead others to Him.

Merriam-Webster's Collegiate Dictionary defines light as "illumination," "spiritual illumination," "inner light," "truth," "enlightenment," and "something that makes vision possible." Light is learning and knowing what you didn't know, being able to see ahead based on what you know, and having a vision of a better future. In Hosea 4:6, God lamented that His people were destroyed because they lacked knowledge. Solomon aptly observed in Proverbs 29:18 (KJV) that "Where there is no vision, the people perish."

Jesus had light. He was light. Divine knowledge was revealed through Him and He had a clear vision of His purpose as well as a vision for the people for whom He was crucified. (See John 14:1-4.) Just as the stars cast light on our physical path, He sheds light on our spiritual being, and His light illuminates our future. It behooves us to follow His example by uncovering the light in us so that others can follow.

Stars represent Christian attributes. The star is more than a beacon of light. As it pierces through dark skies and reaches down to touch the polluted earth beneath, it is not tainted or deterred, let alone destroyed by forces in the earth. From time immemorial, it consistently appears in its season, elegantly performs its duties, and gracefully retires at a set time, only to return when it is called upon again. Order, strength, and faithfulness are among its qualities. Sound like someone you know? The Scripture states that Christ was tempted in all ways, yet he didn't sin (Hebrews 4:15). He excellently performed His mission on earth and retired at the appointed time to sit at the right hand of the Father. Having been called to be like Him, we must cultivate and exhibit these qualities.

More Christian attributes. Have you ever noticed how stars pierce through any weather to reach the earth? Talk about star power! Scientists tell us that depending on location and atmospheric conditions, you can see up to 5,000 stars with the naked eye. On days when the weather is dreadful, it's not unusual to see glimmers of light in the sky, indicating that there are stars on the horizon patiently waiting for the smog to pass. Patience, persistence, and boldness in the face of adversity are remarkable star attributes. Regardless of wind direction, temperature, or the amount of moisture in the atmosphere, stars fearlessly pursue their goal.

In the same vein, Jesus didn't give up His ministry because He was rejected by His own people. Instead, He moved to other places where He found people who willingly received Him. Although He knew Judas was going to betray Him, He didn't conspire to have him killed the day before, nor did He try to sneak out of town by night. Instead, He revealed to His disciples that one of them would betray Him, giving Judas an opportunity to repent or face eternal consequences. Throughout His life on earth, Jesus masterfully weathered all the storms that came His way and triumphantly fulfilled His purpose.

Stars represent the excellence we strive to attain. Stars represent sanctity, excellence, purity, power, beauty, success, victory. Many nations, including the United States, use stars to represent values and key components of their nationalism. Many a poet, writer, singer, scholar, preacher, or politician has employed the star as a symbol of peace, knowledge, strength, authority, respect, love, passion, and grace, to name a few. We speak of four-star hotels and five-star generals and understand them to mean the *crème de la crème* of quality and accomplishment. When you refer to your child as a star student, people advise you to send him or her to an Ivy League college. The term *star* is the preferred accolade for celebrities the world over.

Excellence in any field of endeavor confers a star status. It's hard to imagine a symbol of a higher order. Little wonder that Jesus is known as the Morning Star. Rest assured that there is a star inside of you waiting to blossom. When your talent or gift is fully developed, you will shine as brightly as you can dream.

Stars represent uniqueness. Stars come in all shapes and sizes. Some are round, others flat. The smallest stars are about the size of the earth, and the largest ones are several times that size. While some are relatively close to earth, others are more than twenty trillion miles from it. Each goes by a different name. Though containing similar properties, each is uniquely and beautifully made. First

Corinthians 15:41 gives an accurate description of the great crafts-manship that went into making each star: "The sun has one kind of splendor, the moon another and the stars another; and star differs from star in splendor" (NIV). The same is true of us. Ecclesiastics 3:11 declares that God made everything beautiful, and Psalm 139:14 adds that we were "fearfully and wonderfully made." We should therefore treat every person we meet with respect and dignity. We are all special in the eyes of God.

Stars represent divine wisdom. Stars will always be a mystery. People often wonder how many there are, how far they are, how they were made, how they shine, interact, multiply, survive, etc. Just when we think we've seen them all, scientists report new discoveries. Currently, they estimate that there are ten billion tril-lion stars (10,000,000,000,000,000,000,000) in the Milky Way Galaxy—a rather mind-boggling "star-tistic." Yet there seems to be room for all of them and more. The more of them we can see on any given night, the brighter the night. Instead of warring against one another, they teach us that there's power in numbers, and that we can achieve more as a group than as individuals.

Another mind-blowing revelation: God knows exactly how many stars there are and He calls them all by name (Psalm 147:4; Isaiah 40:26). If He remembers their names, and there are 1.5 tril-lion stars to every human being on earth, you can rest assured that He remembers yours.

When God made a covenant with Abraham, He asked Abraham to look up and count the stars. God then promised him that his offspring would be like the stars, innumerable (Genesis 15:5). But the odds were against Abraham. Here was a one-hundred-year-old man being told that he and his ninety-year-old wife would produce a multitude of descendants (Genesis 17:1-17). Even if they had some variation of ginseng in their time, it still would have been humanly impossible for them to conceive a child. But therein lies a great mystery: *Spiritual principles make little sense from a carnal perspective.* Indeed, the Bible points out that the carnal mind is diametrically opposed to God (Romans 8:7) and that the carnal person cannot receive the things of God because they are spiritual (1 Corinthians 2:14). Abraham submitted himself to God's authority and leadership. He believed God, and the Bible states that God "counted it to him for righteousness" (Genesis 15:6 KJV). He and his wife eventually gave birth to Isaac, from whom the twelve tribes of Israel emerged.

Stars produce stars. When it's time to reproduce, a star will explode into several smaller stars. Each of those baby stars is different and unique in shape, weight, size, and energy level, but the original star DNA remains intact. Similarly, Christ reproduced by choosing twelve men during His earthly ministry. He transformed them so that they became more like Him, although one backslid and was replaced. Before He ascended into heaven, Jesus instructed His followers to make disciples of all nations. But before they began their ministries, they were to wait for power from on high. On the day of Pentecost, the Holy Spirit descended on them and they began to reproduce Christ in others.

Jesus' instruction to His disciples applies to every believer. It's the duty of every child of God to point others to the path of salvation. Filled with the Spirit of God, Daniel prophesied that those who turn others to righteousness will shine like stars forever (Daniel 12:3).

Stars have integrity. Stars seem to command the respect of everything underneath. Why wouldn't they? They have built credibility and proven their trustworthiness over thousands of years by simply being what they were created to be: stars. This was precisely how Christ led His life. From age twelve, He actively began to execute His mission. At no time did He deviate or lose focus. He was faithful in all things till His death. Even the grave could not taint His credibility, as He rose from death on the third day, according to His word. If we want to achieve God's purpose for our lives, we have to be credible Christians.

Stars are fair. Stars have been fair in their dealings with us; they shine on the rich and poor, strong and weak, male and female alike. In the parable of the lost sheep, Christ illustrated what would happen if a shepherd lost one out of a hundred sheep. That shepherd would leave the ninety-nine and go find the one that was lost (Mathew 18:10-14). He would celebrate when the lost sheep was found. Christ was depicting the passion He has for every human being who's not reconciled to the Father. It was for this reason that

He left the comfort of heaven to pay the ultimate price. In addition to treating everyone justly and equitably, it is the duty of every believer to cultivate the same passion for souls.

Stars embody humility. Irrespective of the fact that we gaze at stars with awe-filled eyes and hearts flooded with deep respect, stars are servants, not masters. They assume this servant attitude in a most astonishing manner. Regardless of their size and numerical strength, we are not threatened by them. They are content appearing to us as a bouquet of radiance or luminous twinkles in the face of heaven. How humble!

When the mother of James and John went to Jesus to ask that her sons be allowed to sit at His left and right hands in His kingdom, her request infuriated the other ten disciples. James and John were not the first disciples to be called, probably didn't work any harder than the other disciples, didn't know Jesus before His coming, and were not related to Him by birth. So what grounds did they have to be given such positions of authority in the kingdom of God? Jesus cautioned them by revealing that the greatest among them would be a servant (Mathew 20:27). He Himself came not to be served, but to seek and save those who are lost (Luke 19:10). He later washed their feet to exemplify how they should humble themselves and serve others (John 13:12). By His words and actions, Christ was the originator of the servant-leader model of leadership.

Stars praise their maker. Stars worship and praise their maker. Psalm 145:10 states, "All thy works shall praise thee, O Lord." Psalm 148:3 (KJV) urges the moon and stars to praise Him. Stars continue to do exactly what they were commanded to do at creation. As Samuel rightly counseled Saul, obedience is better than sacrifice (1 Samuel 15:22), and it's the highest form of worship anyone or anything can give. The Morning Star certainly honored his Father in everything; He glorified Him by following through on His purpose. His footprints are there for us to follow.

Stars represent value. The light that stars produce is irreplaceable and plays a significant role in sustaining life on earth. It is so precious money cannot buy it. By the same token, Jesus is worth more than humanity could ever afford. The Bible records that while we were yet sinners, and didn't appreciate the sacrifice He was about to make on our behalf, He willingly gave His life for us (Romans 5:8). Only one word can capture this seemingly irrational decision: *love*. Though He didn't have to do it, and though He wasn't guilty of any sin, He took our sins upon Himself so that someday, if we understood and accepted the truth, we would be like Him.

Divine Empowerment.

Jesus is a superstar! John 1:4 declares that in Him was "life, and the life was the light of men." He proclaimed that He is the light of the world, and that anyone who follows Him shall have the "light of life" (John 8:12).

How does Jesus continue to shine His light even after He was resurrected and returned to His rightful place in heaven? John 1:1 provides the unequivocal answer: "In the beginning was the Word, and the Word was with God and the Word was God." John goes on to add, in verse 14, that "the Word became flesh and dwelt among us, and we beheld His glory, the glory of the only begotten of the Father, full of grace and truth."

Jesus is the Word, and the Word is as forceful and potent today as ever. Before He came to the earth, people inspired by God documented events that foretold His coming. While He was on earth, His disciples documented His life and teachings. All of these writings, which make up the Bible, are for our admonition, instruction, and correction (2 Timothy 3:16). Psalm 119:105 aptly captures how He continues to illuminate our path: "Your word is a lamp to my feet and a light to my path." Jesus continues to live up to His reputation as the Bright and Morning Star!

We must receive the Word of God in our hearts and allow it to renew our minds in order to clearly see the path ahead of us. The stars that are nearest to the earth are more visible than those that are farther away. Although the more distant stars may be several times larger, their luminosity is lost in the distance. The same is true of our relationship with Christ. The more of the Son of God we have in us (by studying, meditating on, and applying the Word), the greater the power of God we will experience. Peter succinctly captured this truth when he said that as we increasingly abide by the Word, the morning star will rise in our hearts (2 Peter 1:19). Jesus will cast a great light on the farthest reaches of your thoughts and dreams if you let Him.

There is more to light than brightness. Scientists tell us that the sun produces enough energy to sustain the earth. Moreover, it provides the gravitational pull that holds the earth in place. Life as we know it would cease to exist without the presence of the sun. The sun was created by God to achieve His purpose. Although it holds the earth in position, it does so at the bidding of the Creator.

By the same token, as many as receive the Son receive the power to be restored as children of God. They receive power over self, sin, and Satan; they receive the power to obtain wealth; they receive supernatural breakthroughs; they receive the sustaining power of God (John 1:12; 1 John 1:9; Mathew 28:18-20; Deuteronomy 8:18). This avalanche of power enables us to become who we were originally created to be.

Are you a star?

Reflect on the presence or absence of the star qualities in your life. Which ones do you easily connect with? Are there any that you have desired but that have constantly eluded you? Are you in position to properly function as a star? Being in position means being connected to the Father through the Son and appropriately applying the Scriptures to your life. Jesus came from heaven to show us the path back to the Father. He was the second Adam; that is, He came to model for us the victorious lifestyle that Adam forfeited when he disobeyed God in the garden.

Reinstating the character, values, and relationship that Adam lost was so important that Christ was willing to make whatever sacrifice was needed. He died on the cross to purchase our freedom, gave His life for ours, gave us joy for sorrow, became poor that we may be rich, was wounded for our sins, was chastised for our peace, and by His stripes, we are healed (Isaiah 53:5). He made all of these sacrifices so we can have a fulfilling life. Although He performed astonishing miracles during His earthly ministry, He said that we will do *greater things* than He did if we believe (John 14:12). There is, therefore, no excuse for any child of God to lead a mediocre life.

CHAPTER 3

Confronting Reality

The future God promises is bright and beautiful. To achieve it, He provides His children with unlimited strength, flawless guidance, boundless favor, impregnable protection, and a guarantee of success.

Deep down in your heart, you see a bright and powerful star eager to shed every hampering weight and show forth the will of the Creator. At the same time, you feel a nauseating discontent with the sin nature and the uncertainty of a godless future. Consequently, you are willing to do whatever it takes to experience salvation, enjoy divine guidance, and achieve your intended future. As you press forward in the right direction, you become convinced that you have a wining combination of vision, energy, and determination.

But moments after you take the first steps, setback strikes; that all-too-familiar sin nature returns with a vengeance. Your latter state seems worse than the former. Reality sets in as you take a guilt trip and wonder why you ever set out to change. Somehow, you muster the courage to proceed, ignoring the dunghill in your path. But soon enough, you fumble into it again. If the right solution is not applied, your effort to better yourself becomes a nightmarish rollercoaster; you're stuck in a swing motion that sucks the fun out of life and leaves you dizzy with stress and tears.

The inescapable truth is that none of us was born perfect. As we mature, the sin nature develops and our strongest passions often become our greatest weaknesses. The Bible points out that we are all tempted by our persistent desires (James 1:14). The teenager who savored the smell of a borrowed cigarette matures into a chain smoker. Along the way, he picks up drugs.

Those for whom smoking and snorting are too off-putting a habit may find that liquor flows like blood in their veins. Just when it appears they're on the verge of a breakthrough, their nemesis gets in the way and they fall right back to where they started. Some give up altogether. They give up everything but the alcohol that's causing their ruin.

Having grown up with inordinate exposure and sensitization to sexuality, others are pitifully trapped in the pangs of lust and sexual immorality. For them, the sanctity of marriage has little meaning.

Another group of people would sell their souls for cash, only to realize that joy and fulfillment are traded in currencies other than money. Yet others lose their heads in the cloud of power. Over time, they realize that all the power in the world cannot redeem their souls.

These vices constitute part of the reality that every one of us has to confront and overcome in the path to the future. Suppressing, repressing, ignoring, or covering them will only cause great harm in the end. Such superficial solutions result in pedophiliac priests, adulterous presidents, and crooked captains of industry, to mention a few recent high-profile examples. Jailhouses across America are teeming with celebrities and failed business leaders. They all managed to circumvent their realities for a time, but inevitably their failures caught up with them.

The problem is spiritual.

Scripture is replete with examples of mortals who confronted diverse realities. By studying their approaches to dealing with their individual situations, we can gain valuable insight into how to overcome our own brutal realities.

The apostle Paul came face to face with reality after he converted to Christianity. After accepting Christ as Lord and Savior, he was poised for a new beginning. However, the sin nature viciously battled his commitment to God. Paul laid it on the line in this passage from the Amplified Bible:

> For I do not understand my own actions [I am baffled, bewildered]. I do not practice or accomplish what I wish, but I do the very thing that I loathe [which my moral instinct condemns].
>
> Now if I do [habitually] what is contrary to my desire, [that means that] I acknowledge and agree that the Law is good (morally excellent) and that I take sides with it.
>
> However, it is no longer I who do the deed, but the sin [principle] which is at home in me and has possession of me.
>
> For I know that nothing good dwells within me, that is, in my flesh. I can will what is right, but I cannot perform it. [I have the intention and urge to do what is right, but no power to carry it out.]
>
> For I fail to practice the good deeds I desire to do, but the evil deeds that I do not desire to do are what I am [ever] doing.
>
> Now if I do what I do not desire to do, it is no longer I doing it [it is not myself that acts], but the sin [principle] which dwells within me [fixed and operating in my soul].
>
> So I find it to be a law (rule of action of my being) that when I want to do what is right and good, evil is ever present with me and I am subject to its insistent demands.
>
> For I endorse and delight in the Law of God in my inmost self [with my new nature].
>
> But I discern in my bodily members [in the sensitive appetites and wills of the flesh] a different law (rule of action) at war against the law of my mind (my reason) and making me a prisoner to the law of sin that dwells in my bodily organs [in the sensitive appetites and wills of the flesh].

> O unhappy and pitiable and wretched man that I
> am! Who will release and deliver me from [the
> shackles of] this body of death? (Romans 7:15-24.)

Paul was caught in a battle that every one of us will have to fight and win if we desire to fulfill God's plans for our lives. Although he understood the will of God and sincerely desired to perform it at all times, his actions did not always match his desire. Like a dog re-ingesting disgorged food, he found himself returning to his old, sinful ways. His best efforts to steer clear of the insatiable sinful appetite that so easily beset him were so thwarted that it caused him great sorrow.

The issue was that, initially, Paul was fighting a spiritual battle with carnal weapons. Most of the people we encounter daily are in a similar situation. They put on a smiley face to mask the battle raging inside. But the naked truth is that we cannot overcome sin by our own strength.

Sin is a spiritual disease, and spiritual ailments can only be cured by spiritual means. Since the sin nature gives the devil access to our lives, he is able to deploy demonic forces that capitalize on our weaknesses, their job being to increasingly pervert the talent God has put in us.

Instead of being a caring and passionate role model, for instance, a teacher can be so perverted by demons he or she begins to lust after underage pupils. If left unchecked, this perversion will continue until it leads to death. Death is one of three rewards the devil offers. The others are loss and destruction (John 10:10).

The spiritual means that can rid us of pathological wrongdoing has to be superior to our problem. As Christ points out, we cannot cast out evil with evil (Luke 11:18). Usually, when demonic torment is in advanced stages, people become desperate for help. They commonly turn to religion for answers. Sadly, there are as many genres of religion as there are shades of color. Many seekers end up with false doctrines or in mystical, mythical, or diabolic circles.

The Bible speaks of the attempt of some exorcists, the seven sons of Sceva, to free a demon-possessed man who sought their help. They had seen the apostle Paul perform various miracles and healings and cast out demons. His actions seemed easy enough to mimic. As with most copycats, they didn't spend the time to learn and apply the truth of what Paul did. During the exorcism, they commanded the demon to come out in the "name of Jesus of whom Paul spoke." They knew the right words and put forth the right act, but lacked the most critical piece: the divine connection. They were incognizant of the fact that the supernatural power that flowed through Paul came through that connection.

Subsequently, the demon spoke through the man, saying, "Jesus I know, and Paul I know, but who are you?" This is evidence of how formidable an enemy Satan is. He knows the Scriptures, can see through your desperate attempts to escape his captivity, and knows when you are applying the right remedy. In this case, the exorcists' ineffectiveness provoked his wrath. After asking the question, the demoniac proceeded to pounce on the men. He beat them so badly they fled the house naked and wounded (Acts 19:11-16). Meanwhile, the demoniac's nightmare only waxed stronger with this experience.

Alcoholics, pathologic thieves, drug and sex addicts, and other people with similar chronic problems often seek help in rehabilitative facilities. For the most part, some of these facilities do a great job of refocusing or retraining these individuals so they can function as normal members of society. Sometimes, they search for triggers or experiences in their patients' lives that engendered the abnormal behavior. The thought is that by addressing those ingrained traumatic triggers, the individual will have a better chance at normalcy. Not infrequently, medication is used during treatment to suppress the undesired behavior.

But these approaches do not address the root cause of the problems. Therapy and medication can only go so far if the sin nature remains dominant. This is where faith-based facilities have a clear advantage. Their emphasis on the spiritual component of a person brings a wholesomeness to their approach that can lead to complete and irreversible restoration.

The solution.
Regardless of what vices have sprouted and become established

in your life, the responsibility for leading a pure and godly life rests squarely with you. The devil is not to blame for persistent woes and failed attempts to break free. God has given you the ability to choose, and He expects you to make the right choice. The good news is that there is a solution that will uproot any malady from its spiritual root and provide enough staying power to prevent recidivism.

Paul, in the same chapter where he bemoaned his fate, found this solution and gave thanks to God (Romans 7:25). He had already made the fundamental choice of accepting Christ into his life. Paul was now being led by the Spirit of God (Romans 8:14). He needed to obey the Spirit by saturating his heart with God's word and by diligently applying it to his life. As the Bible describes, he needed to "work out" or put into practice his salvation (Philippians 2:12).

The Word of God is the sword of the Spirit (Ephesians 6:17). Scripture describes it as "living and powerful" and "sharper than any two-edged sword" (Hebrews 4:12). God made it mighty so it can cut down strongholds (2 Corinthians 10:4). It is the most potent and worthy weapon for fighting vices that have taken root in our lives.

As you fill your heart with the Word, you confront and undo the conditioning of the world. It renews your mind and renders it uninhabitable for Satan and his agents (Romans 12:12). They will have no choice but to leave. The Word of God is light, and darkness cannot withstand it (John 1:5). When you are tempted to indulge, affirm your faith premise by invoking the appropriate Scripture. That will silence the urge.

In addition, cultivate a strong prayer life and remind God of His promises for you; it is scriptural to do so. Replace your deficiency with His sufficiency by claiming those promises. Yes, God's Word is that powerful! If it worked once, it will work again. God hasn't changed; He cannot change (Malachi 3:6). He honors His word, and if you learn to live by it, you will always prevail.

The reality of emotions.

Vices are not the only reality we have to confront. Our emotions—particularly anger, fear, jealousy, and hate—can become a formidable liability if they take control of us. Emotions were originally intended to foster a godly walk and guard against the wiles of the enemy. We are to be angry at the devil and his machinations, fear or revere God, jealously guard our faith, and hate sin. But the sin nature has resulted in the perversion of everything that was intended for good.

Anger. Anger in itself is not sin (Ephesians 4:26). In a noteworthy instance of righteous indignation, Jesus threw out gamblers from a temple. He overturned their tables and cleaned the temple. They had turned the house of God into a haven for thieves and He could not stand by and do nothing (Matthew 21:12-13). As the timeless dictum goes, evil multiplies when good men keep silent. As Christ's ambassadors, we have a responsibility to take constructive action against the onslaught of moral degeneracy.

However, we do not have to be angry to act, as anger can quickly lead to unintended consequences. Knowing how vulnerable we can be, Paul admonishes us to eschew anger altogether (Colossians 3:8). The Scriptures describe God as not easily provoked to anger (Nehemiah 9:17; Psalm 103:8; 145:8; Proverbs 15:18; 16:32). When we consider how much sin is committed in the world every day, God's forbearance might be the only thing standing in the way of Sodom-like consequences.

Moses suffered the effect of succumbing to anger when, in a fit of rage, he murdered an Egyptian who was assaulting a Jew. He probably did not mean to kill the Egyptian, but he ended up with a dead man on his hands. As a result, he lost his position in the court of Pharaoh and escaped into exile. He threw another fit when he came down from Mount Sinai after receiving the Ten Commandments. Upon discovering that the people, under Aaron's leadership, had molded for themselves another god, he slammed to the ground the stones that bore the commandments (Exodus 32:19).

Proverbs 14:17 states that a foolish person is easily provoked to anger. Anger often results in poor decisions, and most people do not want to be around an angry person. In fact, Scripture counsels against friendship with such a person (Proverbs 22:24). Apart from the possibility of becoming the object of his misery, you stand a chance of contracting his hot temper. As the oft-quoted Scripture goes, "Evil communications corrupt good manners" (1 Corinthians

15:33 KJV). It is hard for perennially angry individuals to be prosperous when they continuously repel the people and power that are meant to help them.

The Bible counsels us not to let the sun go down on our anger (Ephesians 4:26). This implies that the cause of anger should be immediately addressed. Harboring and nurturing anger opens a door for the devil. An unforgiving spirit, bitterness, and vengeful thoughts pervade the heart and eventually produce destructive results.

After God accepted Abel's sacrifice but rejected Cain's, Cain held the experience against his brother. His anger resulted in murder. Joseph's brothers' long-standing anger against him almost resulted in his death. Esau was angry and bitter at his brother Jacob for cheating him out of their father's blessing. The anger kept them apart for several years.

Anger produces shame, regret, destruction, and death. After all his heroic efforts, Moses missed the opportunity to enter the Promised Land due to an action that resulted from a moment of fury. Cain became a vagabond and his livelihood was cursed because he lost control of his temper (Genesis 4:12). Joseph's brothers were ashamed to meet him in person after their unconscionable deed. Perhaps you can recall a few instances of rash and regrettable decisions that stemmed from anger. Be thankful that you are still alive. Take the advice in Ecclesiastics 7:9 and teach yourself not to react in anger. In your most tempting moments, whisper a prayer. Ask the Lord to lead you to the right decision. You will be amazed at how He will guide your heart.

There are people who delight in provoking others to anger. They are skilled at finding the right word at the right moment to instigate a susceptible temper. (See Proverbs 15:1.) They anxiously await opportune moments to poke a sore or wink the eye to cause pain and raise tempers. (See Proverbs 10:10.) Such people derive warped pleasure in offending others and causing them to stumble. Abstain from them! Christ said that it would be better if they were thrown into a sea with stones tied around their necks than for them to cause any of his children to stumble (Matthew 18:6; Luke 17:1-2).

Jealousy. Exodus 34:14 commands us not to worship other gods because "the Lord, whose name is Jealous, is a jealous God."

Jealousy in this context does not imply that the Lord would instigate malice against you for acquiring the latest Jaguar or foment a
lawsuit to stall your rise to fame. *Jealous* as the Lord's name
means "zealous." It refers to the zeal of the Lord to protect or
defend His glory and lordship. The Lord warns us in several
Scriptures not to take His name for granted or undermine His
authority because He will jealously defend Himself. (See Exodus
20:5; 34:14; Deuteronomy 4:24; 5:9; 6:15; Joshua 24:19.)

Jealousy as defined above is an attribute that every child of God
should cultivate. The intent is not to share God's glory. Far from it!
The zealousness that stems from it is what we should develop. Not
only does it produce momentum for righteous living, it causes us to
defend all that is precious to us. Moreover, it drives us to seek
justice when moral values are trampled upon.

Having made significant evangelistic efforts in Corinth, Paul
told the Corinthian Christians in a letter that he was jealous over
them with godly jealousy. His desire was that they would preserve
the faith that he had so painstakingly shared (1 Corinthians 11:2).
The book of Proverbs warns men against involvement in adulterous
relationships. It notes that the jealous rage of the man whose
marriage is violated will not abate until justice is done (Proverbs
6:32-35).

On the contrary, the consequences of jealousy when corrupted
can be devastating. When mixed with bitterness, jealousy produces
envy; that is, unjustified resentment toward others. People resent
others for reasons that should have warranted a celebration. They
go one step further by attempting to destroy the source of their jealously. To such people, ultimate satisfaction comes from watching
the person who has aggravated them fall. Saul sought to kill David
because he was envious of David's potential. Joseph's brothers sold
him into slavery because they envied their father's love for him and
detested the possibility of his reigning over them.

The Bible describes envy as the "rottenness of the bones"
(Proverbs 14:30). Pain and destruction are its ultimate offerings. It
is therefore advisable not to allow it in our lives. We can keep envy
out of our lives by embracing the love of God and allowing it to rule
our hearts (1 Corinthians 13:4).

Jealousy can morph into covetousness. *Merriam-Webster's Collegiate Dictionary* defines covetousness as "the inordinate desire for another's possession or for material wealth." It is a monstrous social malaise that has millions of people around the world rushing head over heels to live beyond their means.

Covetous people are the icon of insatiability. Their whole lives are spent in the race to keep up with the Joneses, wear the most expensive jewelry, or acquire whatever their voracious and unmanageable appetites might demand. More often than not, their inordinate desires cause them to indulge in activities that compromise their intended future.

Gehazi and Achan are two biblical personalities who suffered the consequences of a covetous heart. Gehazi was servant to the prophet Elisha. Being sick with leprosy, Naaman, general of the army of Syria, visited Elisha to be healed. Overjoyed with his healing, he offered tantalizing gifts to the prophet as a token of his appreciation. But the prophet would have none of it. As Naaman departed with the gifts, Gehazi mounted his horse in pursuit. When he caught up with Naaman, he said that his master had changed his mind and requested some of the gifts, specifically some money and garments. Naaman generously gave him more than he had asked for. Upon Gehazi's return, Elisha inquired about his whereabouts. He lied again by saying that he had not left the house. Therein lies the biggest problem with deception: one lie always leads to another. As a result of Gehazi's actions, Naaman's leprosy came upon him and his posterity forever (2 Kings 5:15-27).

Under Joshua's leadership, God led Israel in a battle against Jericho. He commanded them to destroy everything in the city except for Rahab and her household. But Achan smuggled some money and garments from the city. His action provoked God's anger against Israel and they consequently lost their next battle with Ai. When Joshua discovered what had happened, Achan and his entire family were stoned to death (Joshua 7:1-26).

Although covetousness holds the promise of instant gratification, the consequences can be life shortening. As Proverbs 28:16 puts it, "He who hates covetousness will prolong his days."

Hate. Hatred is arguably the most powerful emotion. This

emotion should be reserved only for evil and the devil (Proverbs 8:3). We are to hate sin so much that the thought of it repulses us. Sadly, much of humanity's hatred is directed at one another. It has fissured our social fabric into gender, racial, religious, and political patchworks.

Hatred is one of the few destructive emotions that are actively taught and passed down from one generation to another. When it has gained roots, thoughts of the hated entity evoke anger and an urge to harm or destroy it. The stronger the emotion, the greater the temptation to silence the voice of reason. It ultimately results in the destruction of the hater and, sometimes, the hated.

Christ specifically instructs us to love one another as He has loved us (John 13:35). In addition, we are to love our enemies and show kindness to those who hate us (Matthew 5:44; Luke 6:27). If we do not, we will be no better than the unsaved, and we can never be like our heavenly Father (Matthew 5:46). It would be preposterous of us to expect that God would grant our requests for supernatural enablement and guidance when deep down in our hearts we wish to see another human fail.

Once a hateful feeling has been developed, it is hard to eliminate. It took several years before Esau got over the hateful feelings he nursed toward his brother. However, the cleansing Word of God is available to us, and that enables even long-standing hatred to evaporate. However, getting rid of it requires the same level of commitment and the same reconditioning process for overcoming vices. If you are struggling with hatred, take steps *today* to free yourself. By so doing, you will be removing a powerful obstruction to receiving divine empowerment.

Fear. Fear is another emotion that, when perverted, can shackle one down. When the Scriptures speak of fearing God, these verses imply that we have so much reverence for Him that it constrains us from wrongdoing (Proverbs 3:7). That is the reason the psalmist described the fear of God as "the beginning of wisdom" (Psalm 111:10).

Abraham passed a difficult test of obedience because he feared God. (See Genesis 22:12.) When Pharaoh asked the Hebrew midwives to kill every male child at birth, they refused to obey the order because they feared God (Exodus 1:15-17). Shadrach, Meshach, and Abednego refused to worship King Nebuchadnezzar's idol because they feared God (Daniel 3:17-18).

When you fear the Lord with all your heart, you override any other kind of fear, including fear of powerful and wicked people. As Paul rightly noted, you should not be concerned about what people can do to you if God is on your side (Hebrews 13:6).

The midwives would have obeyed the king had he not asked for something that contravened the will of God. They knew they would be putting their lives in jeopardy by disobeying him. This is what the book of Proverbs means when it says that the "fear of man brings a snare" (Proverbs 29:25). If they were fearful of the king, they would have fallen into the trap of murdering innocent children.

The three Hebrew men who refused to worship King Nebuchadnezzar's idol had a similar appreciation for the consequences of their action. Yet they realized that God must take priority in their lives.

The Lord has the ability to cause every situation to favor His faithful children, and He did in all of the above instances.

Perverted fear, on the other hand, effectively arrests progress in any area of one's life that it dominates. When it gains control, it steals attention from the things that count toward one's intended future.

One of the many sources of this sort of fear is guilt. Before Adam and Eve disobeyed God, they often spent time in the garden. But after they ate the forbidden fruit, they were struck by fear and consequently began to hide from God. As the Bible puts it, the wicked run when no one pursues (Proverbs 28:1). Adam and Eve felt insecure, vulnerable, and exposed. Jacob felt the same way after he usurped his brother's blessings. As a result, he fled to a distant city. King Saul choked in fear when he realized that God was with the man he unjustifiably hated. He sought to kill David and lost his throne and life in the process.

It is easier to hide oneself or destroy the object of guilt than to take responsibility for one's actions. People would rather drive bullet-proof cars, surround themselves with physical and electronic walls, and maintain a retinue of bodyguards than humble themselves, take responsibility for their wrongdoing, and make corrections or restitution as necessary. They forget the righteous Judge from whom none of us can hide. He is no respecter of persons, and the only way to avoid His wrath is to confess our guilt and take necessary corrective steps. Whether Adam and Eve would have obtained mercy and therefore a lesser punishment had they taken responsibility for their action will forever remain in the penumbra of doubt. Jacob might not have been tricked into serving fourteen years instead of seven for his wife had he made peace sooner with his brother. And Saul would have died more honorably had he given David a chance.

At a time when Israel was at war, David impregnated Bathsheba, who was married to Uriah, one of his deployed soldiers. Concerned that Uriah might discover his adulterous deed, David had him killed. Then he married Bathsheba.

As far as David was concerned, the matter was over. That was until Nathan confronted him with his sin. God, through Nathan, recounted His blessings on David. He had saved him from Saul and made him king over all of Israel and Judah. If those were insignificant blessings, God said He would have done more for him. Instead of being grateful for all that he had received, David went after the one treasure in an innocent man's life.

Nathan predicted that, as punishment for his action, the child from David's illicit relationship would die. David could have ignored the prophet. He could have had him killed. Instead, he broke down in contrition. For seven days he fasted and prayed for forgiveness and for the life of the child. Although the child died, God consoled David and Bathsheba with Solomon, who became one of the greatest kings in Israel.

It is important to distinguish between a condition of fear, or phobia, and a temporary episode of fear. It is not that one is less harmful than the other; they are both equally destructive. However, approaches to confronting them differ.

Many potential leaders have given up opportunities to climb the corporate ladder for fear of speaking in public, a condition known as phonophobia. Aerophobic people have abandoned blessings for fear of flying. Talented singers have shied away from pursuing their destiny because they are afraid of failure, large audiences, criticism, or success. Fear forces people to accept mediocrity; that is, a way of life that is beneath their potential. I once watched a young lady scamper away from a group of friends who were going to get on an escalator. She was agoraphobic and could not stand the inescapableness of the escalator. She preferred trudging up several flights of stairs to risking a proven and safe technology. In an age where skyscrapers are commonplace, I wondered how high she could go on the stairs.

Life is an expedition and discoveries are made only by steps of faith. Fear denotes the absence of faith, and without faith you will leave many treasures undiscovered. You will never be able to harness the full potential of your talent, let alone tap into supernatural enablement.

Pathologic fear is not of God. The Bible teaches that God did not give us the spirit of fear, but of boldness and a sound mind (2 Timothy 1:7). Proverbs 28:1 adds that "the righteous are bold as a lion." After discovering and developing his gift, Paul explained to the Christians at Ephesus that, after he was saved, he was able to receive a revelation of "the unsearchable riches of Christ" (Ephesians 3:8) that had not been made known to any other human being. Your talent will always produce value for others. And boldness stems from knowing that you are fulfilling God's plan for your life, that you are positively impacting someone else, and that Christ will always be with you so that your efforts produce the right result. Armed with all this knowledge and experience, Paul eagerly and confidently sought to fulfill his purpose (Ephesians 3:1-13).

Take your fears to the almighty God. He calls you to approach His throne with boldness so you may obtain mercy and grace in times of need (Hebrews 4:16). Invite the Spirit of God to fill your heart. He can provide all the freedom you will ever need (2 Corinthians 3:17). Learn to speak the Word to your fear, and trust that God will remove it. He will honor your faith and exchange it for boldness.

Episodic fear, on the other hand, is not connected to any recurring event or thing. It may be caused by a guilty conscience, a traumatic experience, or some kind of threat.

Elijah was a great prophet who performed many miracles. He

resurrected a dead child, provided a supernatural supply of food for the child and his mother, and called down fire from heaven. In keeping with his word to King Ahab, the nation of Judah suffered more than three years of drought.

Yet, when Elijah was threatened by Jezebel, this mighty prophet could not control his fear. He had been obedient in executing judgment on the prophets of Baal (the foreign god of idolatrous Judah). But by so doing, he incurred Jezebel's wrath and she vowed to take his life. Upon hearing the threat, Elijah abandoned his servant and ran as fast as he could into the desert. Curled under a tree, he asked God to take his life (1 Kings 19:4-5). In the grip of fear, he recalled nothing of the indomitable power of the God he served. His faith, testimonies, and knowledge of truth meant little at this point. He was ready to call it quits and abandon whatever was left of God's purpose for his life. Fear will do that to anyone!

Encouragement and guidance are crucial to overcoming episodic fear, and both are gifts that any child of God has the ability to give. When Abraham dismissed his maidservant, Hagar, and his illegitimate child, they wandered for days in the desert of Beersheba until they ran out of food and water. The little boy became frail from dehydration and she feared he would die. But just in the nick of time, an angel appeared. He advised her not to be afraid and guided her to where she could find water (Genesis 21:8-19). You can be the angel that a terrified person somewhere in your path is waiting for. Do not hesitate to help.

Caught between the Red Sea and Pharaoh's army, the people of Israel were gripped with fear. They felt helpless in the face of a life-threatening situation. Nonetheless, they had a leader who had experienced enough of God to know that no situation was too difficult for Him. Moses lifted his voice and counseled the people not to be afraid. He instructed them to stand still and witness the salvation of God. Following his instruction, they crossed the Red Sea and their fear dissipated (Exodus 14:13-30). It is the responsibility of leaders to keep at bay the debilitating effects of fear. This is achieved by ensuring that the root cause of the fear is addressed, not merely its symptoms.

Physical disability as reality.

For some people, reality is a physical disability or disadvantage. It limits their dreams and robs them of the future Scripture promises. But God will accomplish His purpose for your life regardless of your abilities or limitations. You only need to entrust your future to Him and be open to His direction. It may mean developing stronger-than-average faith or going the extra mile, but rest assured that He foreknew that and prepared you for it.

Physical disability. God knew that Moses had a speech problem before selecting him to lead Israel. However, Moses did not immediately see beyond his impediment. Since physical disabilities are a constant presence, it takes a determined effort to see beyond them. Moses spent a great deal of time arguing with God about his future, and had God not intervened, he would have settled for less.

Five biblical women—Sarah, Rachel, Manoah's wife, Hannah, and Elizabeth—had one thing in common: barrenness. Ironically, their destinies were all tied to their children. Sarah and Abraham had been promised a child by God, but years went by and they had none. In her anxiety, Sarah sought a shortcut to her intended future by persuading Abraham to have a child by their servant Hagar. Ishmael was the product of that extramarital relationship. When Isaac was finally born, Ishmael became a source of friction, and he and his mother were eventually separated from Abraham's family. That separation was excruciating for Abraham, as he loved Ishmael. The agony continued long after their departure. This is what can happen when, by reason of a limitation, we compromise our position. (See Genesis 21:1-14.)

Rachel and her sister Leah were married to Jacob. Rachel watched in sorrow as her sister bore seven children. It was such a painful experience that Rachel considered suicide. But she did not have to experience all that agony. She could have exerted faith and waited patiently. God had a perfect plan for her life. Not only would she bear children, but she was going to bear the vice president of a renowned nation. All of Leah's sons would later honor Joseph, one of Rachael's two sons, as king (Genesis 30:1, 22-24; 42:6).

An angel visited Manoah's wife, told her she would have a child, and provided instructions on how the child should be raised. She heartily received the message and shared it with her husband. Being a faithful man of God, Manoah supported his wife and prayed for the angel to visit again. They eventually had Samson, who judged Israel for twenty years (Judges 13:1-25; 16:31). Manoah and his wife are great examples of how a disabling condition should be handled. They were able to avoid the distress that their condition could have brought by trusting their situation to God.

Hannah provides another instance of God intervening in a situation so that His purpose might be accomplished. She was a devout and prayerful woman, but she lived several years without a child. Like Rachel, she had a mate for whom childbearing was not an issue. After enduring years of taunting and name-calling, Hannah received the answer to her prayers.

Do not allow people to pressure you into making a bad decision. Your future is not in their hands. When the omniscient One comes through for you, the breakthrough that will follow will confound your detractors. Hannah gave birth to Samuel, who became a judge over Israel (1 Samuel 1:1-20; 7:15).

Elisabeth is a particularly interesting case. She and her husband, Zacharias, a priest, led righteous lives before God. They were both old and had no child. During one of the nights that he served in the temple, the angel Gabriel appeared and told him that he would have a son. The son would be Christ's forerunner. He told him the son's name, John, and shared details about his ministry. Although Zacharias was a devout priest, he did not quite believe the angel of God. He asked for a sign as proof. Appalled at his unbelief, the angel rendered him dumb. There are consequences to doubting God. We are much better, safer, and wiser if we take Him at His word. Zacharias did not speak until the day John was born. Jesus said John was the greatest of all men (Luke 1:5-20; Luke 7:28). I'm sure Elisabeth and Zacharias considered their son well worth the wait!

God had something unique and extraordinary for each of these barren women. The successes of their children far surpassed their imaginations. The joy that resulted outweighed the agony of waiting several forlorn years. And their enemies were silenced for good. If you find yourself in a similar situation, take solace in their experiences. *Your salvation is nearer than you think.*

The sufficiency of grace. Sometimes your condition does not have to change for you to be victorious. Paul spoke of an infirmity in his body. He described it as a "thorn in the flesh" (2 Corinthians 12:7) and prayed to God three times for healing, but healing never came. God could have cured him. But He had given Paul so many revelations that he could easily have become prideful. The infirmity was to keep him in check. It was a constant reminder that God was the source of his runaway success.

Christ underscored this point in His response to Paul: "My grace is sufficient for you." He added that His grace is made perfect in weakness (vs. 9).

Grace is unmerited favor that is able to surpass every personal weakness to produce the perfect will of God in your life. When that disease, pain, reproach, concern, or oddity you have been praying about does not disappear, do not let it slow you down. Pray for grace to come on you. It will make you unstoppable.

Physical disadvantage. Zacchaeus, a tax collector, demonstrated how to overcome personal disadvantage. As Christ's fame spread far and wide, throngs of people followed everywhere He went. Zacchaeus wanted desperately to meet the Savior, but he was so short he could easily be lost in the crowd. He therefore took an unusual and creative step to meet with Christ. Knowing Jesus would be passing a particular road, he went ahead of Him and climbed a tree so he could see the Messiah. When Jesus got there, He looked up, saw his faith, and asked him to climb down from the tree. Instead of just a passing encounter on a highway, the Messiah went with Zacchaeus to his house. That same day, Zacchaeus gave his life to Christ (Luke 19:2-10).

There is always opportunity in our adversity, and it will not elude us if we look hard enough. God will exceed your expectations when you reach out in faith.

Age as reality.

For some people, age can pose the biggest stumbling block in the face of a life-changing opportunity. The world system divides the human life span into segments of "normal" and "sensible" actions, behaviors, and accomplishments. For example, it is perfectly "normal" for five-year-olds to be first graders and eighteen-year-olds to be college freshmen. It's "unusual" for a teenager to be a college professor and weird for a sexagenarian to be pregnant.

Contrary to the clichéd Latin maxim, *vox populi* (the voice of the people) is not always *vox Dei* (the voice of God). If anything, the Word declares that God does not reason the way humans do. He said that as the heavens are higher than the earth, so His thoughts and ways are higher than our thoughts and ways (Isaiah 55:9). He created us for His purpose and therefore reserves the right to order our lives as He deems fit.

From the unborn child to the great-grandparent, Scripture provides instances of how divine purpose transcends age. God can and does use people of any age to accomplish His purpose. It was not by accident that Esau and Jacob struggled in their mother's womb. Their hyperactivity was God's way of using them to get Rebekah's attention. The twins represented two distinct and great nations, and God thought it necessary to advise her in advance (Genesis 25:23).

When God called Jeremiah to deliver a message to rebellious Judah, Jeremiah argued that he was but a child. He might have pondered the reaction of thousands of people to what was to be a mostly sad and defeatist message. His life could have been in danger. Moreover, the people could have made light of his message due to his young age. But God had already told him that he had been appointed a prophet before he was formed in his mother's womb. God has predetermined the future of each and every one of us!

Jeremiah needed to make a destiny-shaping decision and he made the right one. God subsequently reached out and touched his mouth, imparting divine enablement. Age was never again a factor in his successful ministry (Jeremiah 1:5-9).

We must always remember that our destinies are not about how much we can achieve by our strength, but how willing we are to allow God to accomplish His will through us. The latter yields the fulfillment that we earnestly desire.

Amon, as king of Judah, deviated from the ways of God. He perpetuated the idolatry that his father had established. Dismayed by his leadership, his servants conspired and murdered him. Upon his death, Josiah, his eight-year-old son, was named king.

Despite his tender age, the Bible records that in all thirty years of Josiah's reign, "he did that which was right in the sight of the Lord, and walked in all the way of David his [fore]father, and turned not aside to the right hand or to the left" (2 Kings 22:2 KJV). Josiah succeeded where his father failed, not because of his physical abilities, but because he put God first in his life.

As a teenager, David had the faith, boldness, and wisdom to defeat the Philistine army. In their youth, Shadrach, Meshach, and Abednego made such powerful public demonstrations of their faith that they caused an entire nation to acknowledge and reverence the God of Abraham, Isaac, and Jacob.

The next time your teenage child or sibling draws back from an obvious calling, remind him or her that Jesus was only twelve when He launched a successful ministry. At that tender age, His wisdom surpassed the collective wisdom of the rabbis who had ministered for years in the synagogues. The same power that worked in and through Him is available to you.

Aging. Aging is a limitation engendered by the sin nature. Had the first couple not sinned, Botox might mean something different today. God is ageless, timeless, and unchanging. At age ninety, Sarah thought it was ridiculous to conceive and bear a child. But that was God's chosen time and He thought she was a worthy vessel.

It is pointless to worry about what others think when God is orchestrating His will for your life. People who saw Sarah's protruding abdomen might have considered it a disease or a byproduct of aging. But God was incubating a huge blessing. Sarah could have been concerned about her health and ability to sustain a pregnancy for nine months. Our sense-making approach to life would suggest that she was at great risk. But God never does any work halfway. Retired or tired, if he has called you, He will amply supply the strength for the job.

Social realities.

Economic, social, and political realities may be the handicaps you face as you reach for your dream. It may seem preposterous for jejune paupers to dream of owning a prosperous business or for plebs to aspire to royalty. But then again, status and wealth are not a part of God's selection criteria.

When He sent Samuel to Jesse's house to anoint a king for Israel, God did not disclose beforehand which of Jesse's sons was to be anointed. Samuel asked Jesse to gather his sons so they could be sanctified in preparation for the selection. As they came, Samuel saw Eliab, one of the sons, and thought he would be the king. He was tall, handsome, and well dressed. By the prophet's estimation, he certainly looked the part. Nevertheless, God cautioned him against looking on outward appearance. Seven of Jesse's sons came by and He did not pick any of them. Worried at the development, Samuel called Jesse aside and asked if he had another child. Only in that moment did it occur to him that his youngest son was in the field tending to his flock. No one had thought about him, probably because he was a young, classless shepherd who spent much of his time working in the fields. On the other hand, he gave his best effort to whatever he was asked to do. He was content to shepherd the family's flock by himself. His humble attitude put him in a position where God could prepare him for his future. In the end, he was selected to lead Israel.

God does not just give you a vision; He makes provision for the vision. David did not have to beg to be appointed king. He did not plot to overthrow Saul, the reigning king. Even when Saul turned against him, he never lost his focus. God gave him Samuel and Nathan as guides and mentors. Everything he would ever need to ascend to the throne had been providentially assigned.

Before you discount yourself as a nonentity, remember that Christ gave His life for everyone. His goal was to restore everything that the Father had planned for your future. As Christ said of Himself, let it be said of you that the stone the builders rejected has become the cornerstone (Matthew 21:42). Wipe the dust off your dreams and begin afresh the quest of your soul. Avail yourself of every opportunity to do good work, and in due time, your breakthrough will come.

Temporal limitations.
There is hardly any grown-up in America who is not pressed for

time. Some people are so regimented that they are scheduled for years in advance. Now, there is great value to being organized. The history of creation gives us an insight into the decency and order that characterize God's work.

However, God's plan for you may not always fit with your schedule. And hesitation and procrastination can derail your destiny.

You have to be open and flexible to God's direction. He did not give Phillip any prior notice when He asked him to meet with the Ethiopian statesman (Acts 8:26). Had Phillip hesitated, the statesman might not have been saved.

God in his infinite mercy sent His angels to lead Lot and his family out of Sodom and Gomorrah. But Lot's wife hesitated and never made it out.

When God asked Noah to build an ark, there was no proof that it might rain so much that the whole earth would be flooded. But had he ignored God's instruction, he and his family would have died in the flood.

Do not let the things you see or do not see deter you from actively pursuing the vision the Lord has given you. It is better to obey Him and face the ridicule of the world than to disobey Him and suffer the consequence.

Jesus taught a lesson on prioritization when He visited with Mary and Martha. Mary chose to sit and hear Christ's message of life, but Martha was preoccupied with all the preparation that had to be made to ensure that their guest was comfortable. When Mary did not join her, she complained to Jesus and asked Him to tell Mary to join her in serving. The response she received is something we all can learn from: "Martha, Martha, you are worried and upset about many things, but only one thing is needed. Mary has chosen what is better, and it will not be taken away from her" (Luke 10:41-42 NIV).

Apart from the lost opportunities that result from misplaced priorities, people who are concerned with doing too many things hardly get anything done. Your blessings do not consist in engaging in many activities; they consist in engaging in the right activities.

Conclusion.

Your future is too important to allow obstacles to get in the way. If you have been struggling in any area of your life, now is the time to apply what you have learned. Do not stop until you have been completely freed.

Spiritual Development

CHAPTER 4

Faith Premise

Faith is a nonnegotiable prerequisite for a relationship with God. The Bible states that "without faith it is impossible to please Him" (Hebrews 11:6). None of us has seen God. He is a spirit and requires that those who worship Him do so "in spirit and in truth" (John 4:24). No matter how hard we try, we cannot reach Him by our own works. Faith is the spiritual vehicle that connects us to Him.

We cannot achieve our full potential without a healthy relationship with God. If faith is the means by which we can reach Him, it behooves us to understand what it is and learn how it can work for us.

Faith is gospel truth.

The word *faith* originates from the Greek word *pistis,* which means "religious truth or conviction." It is especially understood as reliance upon Christ for salvation. It is belief, assurance, and confidence in the existence and truthfulness of God.

Faith gives us access to God's unlimited power (Romans 5:2). And that power enables us to do everything He has purposed for us (Philippians 4:13).

Faith principles are usually unpopular (John 7:7). They often contradict the ways of the world. This is due to the fact that God's ways are not our ways. For instance, He sees and knows the end of everything even before it begins. Thus, He is able to act boldly and decisively, knowing precisely what the outcome will be. A faithless person cannot operate with such certainty because he goes only by what he can see and project. At best, considering that there are always forces beyond our control, his projections are an educated guess. Our future is too important to be subjected to mere guesswork.

Faith takes the guesswork out of our future. We are able to receive from God a clear vision of what we should be doing, as well as the guidance and resources to get it done.

Faith at work.

The Bible states that those who come to Christ must believe that He exists and that "He is a rewarder of those who diligently seek Him" (Hebrews 11:6). You cannot receive God's blessings without faith. You will always receive what you believe.

Two blind men, wanting to be healed, called out to Jesus for help. When He turned around, He asked if they believed He could heal them. When they responded in the affirmative, He touched their eyes and said, "According to your faith, let it be to you" (Matthew 9:27-29). Had the men not believed in the healing power of God, it would not have worked for them.

Many of us seek God's help today. However, if our prayers and supplications are not grounded in faith, we will not experience the desired result. Faith clears the way for the power of God to reach you.

Some people seem to relish negativism. They frequently confess their conviction that nothing ever works well for them or in their environment. This belief system is so detrimental that not even God can help them. Until they change their belief system, miracles will always elude them.

Faith enables you to overcome and transcend your natural limitations. It is the means by which you can tap into God's power and achieve supernatural results. As a teenage shepherd, David had received no training in the art of war. However, he had had experiences that built up his faith in the Lord. While watching his father's flock, God divinely empowered him so that he was able to hunt down and destroy the wild beasts that attacked the sheep. So when he saw Goliath, a nine-foot-plus Philistine bully, defying the God of

Israel, he was ready to put his faith to work.

At first, Saul, the king, was in disbelief. But after David shared his experiences with the wild animals, Saul hesitantly authorized him to confront the enemy. When the soldiers put their protective gear on David, it was so heavy he could not move. So he took it off. God was setting up the situation so there would not be any question as to who defeated Goliath.

Having experienced God move in the past, David understood that the battle was not his to fight. He was so confident in his source of strength that he insisted on confronting a seasoned warrior without any body armor or weapons except for five stones and a sling. To the utter amazement of soldiers on both sides, he brought down the giant by slinging a stone into his temple (1 Samuel 17:49). Clearly, the victory was beyond David's natural abilities. But faith made all the difference.

Faith reverses impossibilities. Matthew 9:20 details the story of a woman who had hemorrhaged for twelve years. During those years, she spent everything she had trying to get cured. She had endured several embarrassing moments and diverse medical interventions to no avail. But when she heard that Jesus was coming to town, she lit up her faith. It was so strong that she did not think it necessary to even speak with Him. "If only I may touch his clothes, I shall be made well" (Mark 5:28). When the opportunity came, she touched the hem of Christ's garment, and instantly, her faith was honored and she was healed.

Christ declares that all things are possible to those who believe (Mark 9:23). *There are no exceptions.* No matter how ugly or desperate a situation may be, it is subject to this spiritual principle of infinite possibility.

Faith supplies needs you cannot meet. Testing Abraham's faith, God asked him to sacrifice his son, Isaac. As they were going up to the altar to make the sacrifice, Isaac said to his father, "The fire and wood are here, but where is the lamb for the burnt offering?" (Genesis 22:7 NIV). If there was a time in his life that Abraham could have had second thoughts, this was it. But he responded by faith and told Isaac, "God himself will provide the lamb for the burnt offering" (Genesis 22:8 NIV). Just in the nick of time, God provided a lamb for the offering (Genesis 22:11-12).

Just as He did with Abraham, God has already made available everything you need to achieve your purpose. Faith is the surefire means by which you can reach out and take it.

Faith always brings more blessings than are needed. Paul wrote in his letter to Ephesus that God is able to do "exceedingly abundantly above all that we ask or think" (Ephesians 3:20). All that Abraham needed was a lamb, and God provided one. But because he was faithful, God also proclaimed the following blessing on his life: "Because you have done this thing, and have not withheld your son, your only son, blessing I will bless you, and multiplying I will multiply your descendants as the stars of the heaven and as the sand which is on the seashore; and your descendants shall possess the gate of their enemies. In your seed all the nations of the earth shall be blessed, because you have obeyed My voice" (Genesis 22:16-18). Abraham could not have anticipated what God had in store for him.

Jesus knew what faith can do when He was confronted with five thousand hungry men. Having been following and listening to Him for a long while, the crowd was hungry. Moved with compassion, He asked His disciples what food was available, and they only came up with five loaves of bread and two fishes. For Jesus, that was more than enough.

After He blessed the fish and bread, it fed five thousand men, not counting women and children, and they had twelve baskets left over (John 6:1-13). All that God asks of us is to trust Him with what little talents or ideas or resources we have so that He may bless and multiply them.

Faith will cause forces to work in your favor. Before Paul had a life-changing experience on his way to Damascus, he was a notorious persecutor of Christians. His reason for going to Damascus was to arrest and punish them for their faith. He was causing so much havoc for the disciples that they needed God to intervene.

A talented lawyer and leader, Paul (then Saul) was abusing the talent and zeal the Lord had put in him. But Jesus accosted him on the way to Damascus and revealed to him the way of life. That experience transformed him from a persecutor of believers to a preacher of the gospel. In the end, faith caused him to achieve what he could never have achieved as an unbeliever. Not only did he write most of the New Testament, he did more to spread the gospel to the Gentiles than all the other apostles.

The Scriptures note that "all things work together for good to those who love God" (Romans 8:28). The person or power standing in your way does not matter. If you take hold of this promise by faith, everything will work out in your favor.

Daniel, Shadrach, Meshach, and Abednego were Jews who lived in Babylon under King Nebuchadnezzar at the time of the Babylonian exile. Though they were foreigners, God favored them so much that they were appointed counselors to the king. However, they needed to undergo a period of preparation before they could assume their roles. They were supposed to be fed special food and wine during this period so they would be "fattened up" for their confirmation meeting with Nebuchadnezzar.

But Daniel and his friends knew the king's food and wine would defile them, and they refused to make that sacrifice. So they declined the king's offer. This caused the prince to worry that they would not look good enough when it came time to present them to the king. He was also concerned that the king would kill him as a result. But Daniel assured him that all would be well.

In an attempt to steer clear of the king's wrath, the prince tested the four Hebrew men by allowing them to go on their own diet for ten days. At the end of that trial period, much to his surprise, they looked better than the people who had been eating the king's food. When they finally met the king, he found them so knowledgeable, wise, and intelligent that he proclaimed them *ten times better* than the magicians and astrologers in all of his kingdom (Daniel 1:1-20). As a testimony to divine enablement, even a captor-king acknowledged and rewarded their excellence.

On a different occasion, Nebuchadnezzar did something that strained his relationship with Shadrach, Meshach, and Abednego. He made an idol and required everyone in his kingdom to worship it. However, the Hebrew trio refused to commit idolatry. They were again asserting their faith. But this time, their lives were at stake.

The king gave them the opportunity to rescind their decision but they remained defiant. When he threatened to cremate them alive, they replied that their God would deliver them, but that even if He did not, they would not bow to the idol. Enraged by their response, the king commanded that the furnace be heated seven times hotter than usual.

When you take a stand for the Lord, do not be surprised if your enemy, the devil, throws all his weight at you to tempt your faith. He would like nothing more than to discredit your faith before a watching world. Give him no chance!

At the king's command, soldiers threw the three Hebrew men into the fire, which was so blazing hot it killed all the men who threw them in it. This is a lesson to those who lend themselves as instruments to the enemy to seek the downfall of a child of God. God said He will be an enemy to your enemy (Exodus 23:22). So you can be assured, your enemies will never prevail against you.

When the king summoned the courage to glance into the furnace, he was flabbergasted by what he saw. The Hebrew men were at ease in it! What's more, there was a fourth man in there, and in the king's words, "the form of the fourth is like the Son of God" (Daniel 3:25). In honoring the faith of the Hebrew men, God caused an inferno to work in their favor.

Christ was not being figurative when He promised to be with us in every situation. He is "a very present help" in trouble (Psalm 46:1). David wrote that even though he walked "through the valley of the shadow of death," he would not fear evil because the Lord would be there with him (Psalm 23:4).

Daniel was not accused in the fiery furnace experience, but his trial was sure to come. After Nebuchadnezzar's death, Darius assumed kingship in Babylon and promoted Daniel to one of three governorship positions. This caused jealousy among the locals and they conspired against Daniel. They knew he was a prayerful man and that he prayed openly three times daily. So they asked the king to sign a decree that everyone in his domain must pray to him for thirty days.

The enemy will go to ridiculous lengths to find fault with you. In his way of thinking, anything that hurts, limits, undermines, or destroys you is rational and acceptable.

The king signed the decree but Daniel maintained his prayer

tradition. All the power in the world was not worth damaging his relationship with the Lord. He was consequently arrested and thrown into a lion's den.

Daniel was in the den with the wild beasts for one whole night but his safety was not at all compromised. The king, on the other hand, was troubled all night. He had wrongfully accused and punished an innocent man, and deep down in his heart, he hoped Daniel would somehow survive the punishment. Very early the next morning, he rushed to the den, and to his delight, he found Daniel alive. Daniel's God had come through for him! He ordered the men who had accused him to be thrown into the den along with their families. God put back on the devil what he had intended for His child. If need be, He will do the same for you.

King Darius rewarded Daniel by promoting him to his second-in-command, and he decreed that "the God of Daniel" be feared and worshipped in his kingdom (Daniel 6:1-26). Once more, God caused what would have been a deadly situation to work out in His child's favor. I do not imagine that your situation could be worse than these examples. If God came through for them, he will come through for you!

Faith commands enough power to transform any situation. Jesus said that if we have faith as small as a mustard seed, we can command a mountain to move and it will obey (Matthew 17:20). Take a moment to consider that statement. Are there any mountains in your life? Do any of these sound familiar: chronic illness, barrenness, joblessness, poverty, instability? You have the power to overcome all of them. God did not intend for you to suffer all your life under the weight of problems and diseases. The Bible declares that His thoughts toward you are thoughts of good, not of evil, to give you an expected end (Jeremiah 29:11). Stand on this promise by faith. Since God always honors faith, you can be assured that your situation will not hang around for long.

Take a faith stand.

Hebrews 11:1 reveals that "faith is the substance of things hoped for, the evidence of things not seen." It follows that you have to be hoping for something to exercise faith. You are not exercising faith when you allow events and circumstances to dictate how you live. Indeed, you can never achieve your full potential that way, as you will be incessantly tossed around by competing forces.

Your starting point is to take a stand for your life. You are not on the earth by accident. You are not one of six billion people; you are one in six billion people! In other words, you are specially and uniquely made, with a divinely appointed purpose. You are a star, and your light is critical to the world you live in. Therefore, you have to make up your mind to be all that your Creator intended for you to be. You must believe that no power is capable of stopping or derailing you.

Defend your faith.

Since faith is so crucial to our lives, the devil will exploit every possible means to prevent us from putting our faith in God. If we beat him and establish a relationship, he will strive to compromise or annul it. This is why Jude advises us to defend our faith (Jude 1:3).

In order for us to defend our faith, God's Word must fill our hearts. There is an answer for every situation, and we do not want to be without it in the heat of battle. Christ overcame all the temptations the devil threw his way because He had a word for each of them (Luke 4:1-13).

The "good fight of faith" (1 Timothy 6:12), as Paul describes it, is a battle you cannot lose. Faith doubles as an impregnable shield and body armor in your fight with the devil (Ephesians 6:16; 1 Thessalonians 5:8). Regardless of what challenges he throws your way, confess the Word and victory will always be yours!

Final thoughts.

We exercise more faith every day than we realize. Our relationships could not function without it. In friendship, business, and politics, we make plans and set goals, and our success in those areas often rests on resources that are not yet available or on people we barely know. However, we trust that at a predetermined future date, those resources or people will be available. This is faith in action.

Faith is at work whenever an entrepreneur risks his or her future on a business plan. It is at play when a venture capitalist looks at that plan and decides to commit millions of dollars in the hope of making a profit. It is present when you meet a complete stranger and several months later the two of you decide to spend the rest of your lives together. You exercise faith when you get on an airplane and trust your life to a pilot you have never met. Faithlessness would be a state of paralysis.

Christ teaches that there are degrees of faith, and if you want to be a star, your faith needs to be strong enough to withstand significant obstacles and opposition.

Trust is the essence of a faith-based relationship. It is the belief that a future action or event will conform to predetermined terms. Unfortunately, trust is breached so frequently that it carries negligible weight with many people. It is especially difficult for those whose trust has been breached to get back into the habit of trusting. But as the Bible teaches, we create this difficulty for ourselves by putting our trust in the wrong places. Psalm 118:8 says, "It is better to trust in the Lord than to put confidence in man." Psalm 34:8 adds that "Blessed is the man who trusts in Him." Proverbs 3:5 advises that we trust in the Lord with all our heart. This is important because human beings fail, and sometimes, they fail when you least expect.

God's faithfulness cascades down the waterfall of eternity. If you commit your family and friends, your job, your coworkers and colleagues, and the circumstances you encounter into His hands, you will never be disappointed. For even when they fail, God will cause their failure to work in your favor.

CHAPTER 5

The Power of Thinking

The entire world is evidence that God thinks *big*! Heaven is His dwelling and the earth His footrest. As advanced as science has become, it is not close to fathoming the scope of God's creative work throughout the universe. Scientists have settled for a yearly bouquet of discoveries. However, the source and reaches of the flowers they harvest every so often are simply incomprehensible.

When the psalmist pondered God's greatness and magnificence, he wondered why He would be so mindful of us (Psalm 8:4). But as we see in Jeremiah 29:11, not only does He think about us, His thoughts toward us are *good thoughts* and are meant to grant our wishes. Believers can tap into the promise of this Scripture and bring great success into their lives.

Joshua tapped into it and consequently enjoyed spectacular success as a warrior and leader. After Moses died, God appointed Joshua leader of Israel. He was to lead Israel through several treacherous territories into the Promised Land. Needless to say, it was a Herculean task, and Joshua could not have completed it alone. Though he knew God would always be there for him, and would ultimately lead him to success, he needed to understand God's ways so he could walk in them diligently.

God therefore gave him an infallible formula for success. It is a formula that should be familiar to people who aspire to achieve their full potential. He instructed Joshua to think (or meditate) on the laws and promises He had given Moses. He emphasized that he was to do so day and night. God wanted to ensure that His word was ingrained in Joshua. That was the only way he could make the right decisions in all the battles that awaited him. Moreover, the promises were to remind him that he was not alone in the journey and that there was light at the end of the tunnel.

Like Joshua, you will encounter challenges as you navigate your destiny. However, if you meditate on God's Word often, and allow it to guide your actions, you will never have cause to doubt. Better yet, you will always emerge victorious.

Consider meditating on the promises below from Deuteronomy 28:1-14 (AMP):

> If you will listen diligently to the voice of the Lord your God, being watchful to do all His commandments which I command you this day, the Lord your God will set you high above all the nations of the earth.
>
> And all these blessings shall come upon you and overtake you if you heed the voice of the Lord your God.
>
> Blessed shall you be in the city and blessed shall you be in the field.
>
> Blessed shall be the fruit of your body and the fruit of your ground and the fruit of your beasts, the increase of your cattle and the young of your flock.
>
> Blessed shall be your basket and your kneading trough.
>
> Blessed shall you be when you come in and blessed shall you be when you go out.
>
> The Lord shall cause your enemies who rise up against you to be defeated before your face; they shall come out against you one way and flee before you seven ways.
>
> The Lord shall command the blessing upon you

in your storehouse and in all that you undertake. And He will bless you in the land which the Lord your God gives you.

The Lord will establish you as a people holy to Himself, as He has sworn to you, if you keep the commandments of the Lord your God and walk in His ways.

And all people of the earth shall see that you are called by the name [and in the presence of] the Lord, and they shall be afraid of you.

And the Lord shall make you have a surplus of prosperity, through the fruit of your body, of your livestock, and of your ground, in the land which the Lord swore to your fathers to give you.

The Lord shall open to you His good treasury, the heavens, to give the rain of your land in its season and to bless all the work of your hands; and you shall lend to many nations, but you shall not borrow.

And the Lord shall make you the head, and not the tail; and you shall be above only, and you shall not be beneath, if you heed the commandments of the Lord your God which I command you this day and are watchful to do them.

And you shall not turn aside from any of the words which I command you this day, to the right hand or to the left, to go after other gods to serve them.

The transparency of human thoughts.

Our thoughts, even the remotest of them, are transparent to God (Psalm 94:11; Matthew 6:8; 9:4; Luke 11:17). We cannot hide them from Him (Job 42:2). God, unlike humans, considers the heart in executing judgment (1 Samuel 16:7). He knows that every action originates from a thought, so if the thought process is in accordance with His Word, the resulting action will be right.

Before the devil was cast out of heaven, God saw the covetous thought in his heart (Isaiah 14:13-15). Satan thought about exalting himself above the other angels and being like God. He never had a chance to share that thought!

When Christ was born, King Herod thought about killing Him so He would not pose a threat to his kingdom. But that was not what he told the wise men from the east. God, being omniscient, saw his thoughts and intervened (Matthew 2:1-14).

When Jesus observed a group of worshipers as the offering basket was being passed around, He saw a widow who gave a penny. He later told His disciples that the widow gave more than all the other givers. Christ had discerned her thoughts and knew that the woman gave all she had (Luke 21:1-3).

Thought process for believers.

If we want God's blessings to operate in our lives, if we earnestly desire to experience all He has purposed for us, we must follow His requirement for our thought process. Paul articulates these requirements in this statement: "Whatever things are true, whatever things are noble, whatever things are just, whatever things are pure, whatever things are lovely, whatever things are of good report, if there is any virtue and if there is anything praiseworthy— meditate on these things" (Philippians 4:8).

This is not an easy task, primarily because the human heart is naturally devious. As Jeremiah put it: "The heart is deceitful above all things, and desperately wicked; who can know it?" (Jeremiah 17:9). The deceitfulness and wickedness of the heart are consequences of the sin nature. However, we have the ability to choose what we meditate on. When corrupt or unwholesome thoughts crop up in our hearts, we can assert our authority as children of God and override those thoughts (2 Corinthians 10:5). We can keep poisonous thoughts at bay by renewing our minds (Colossians 3:10; Ephesians 4:23). We renew our minds by constantly meditating on God's Word. The psalmist put it eloquently: "Your word I have hidden in my heart, that I might not sin against You" (Psalm 119:11).

Christians must cultivate the habit of thinking critically. (See Philippians 4:8.) For instance, if you get a sudden urge to buy a boat, or to invite your secretary out to dinner, it helps to pause and validate the thought in light of Scripture. Why do you want a boat? Is it because John Q down the street bought one last month? Do you know how much Mr. Q makes annually? More important, have you sought God's will on the boat? And as for your secretary, you have always admired her sense of fashion and wanted to tell her so. But what message would you be sending if you did? Where would it lead? How would your wife react if she knew you were taking this woman out to dinner?

The type of critical thinking described in Philippians 4:8 helps us not to make stupid decisions. Many thoughts may seem innocuous on the surface, but once you hatch them, you discover they are a ride to hell. Do not be a victim.

The necessity of aligning thought.

It is absolutely necessary for your thoughts to be aligned with God's will because there is an adversary who wants to take control of your life, and if he succeeds, he will lead you down the wrong path. As the Bible states, you cannot serve two masters. You will have to submit to one or the other (Matthew 6:24).This means you are either operating by the Word of God or by the ways of the world.

God wants the best for you. He knows the world, being Satan's domain (John 12:31), will not teach you His ways. While He requires absolute truth, Satan relishes moral relativism. Though He forbids sin, Satan thrives on it. It is an ongoing spiritual warfare to win hearts, and people often succumb to what they consider the easy way.

The Bible teaches that there is a way that seems right to us, but the end of it is destruction (Proverbs 14:12). I'm sure you would agree that destruction is not the future God intended for you. You must therefore allow Him to guide your thinking. There is no third option. If there was, God would have offered it.

We are what we think.

Proverbs 23:7 teaches that we are what we think. Our lives today are the cumulative result of our thought patterns. Trials, temptations, and tragedies occur to prevent us from becoming all that God purposed for us to be. These circumstances are often beyond our control. It is therefore easy for them to become an excuse.

But God does not accept excuses. He has made and given us everything we need to live victoriously. He affirms that nothing can separate us from His love (Romans 8:35) and that we will always triumph in Christ (2 Corinthians 2:14). He has promised to create an escape for us from every temptation (1 Corinthians 10:13). Our success rests on how we apply His Word to our thoughts. If we become adroit at meditating on and appropriating His Word in our lives, nothing can stand in our way.

All of life's decisions are made by thinking.

The world is replete with sundry information. Some pieces of information are useful; others are downright destructive. Thinking is how we sift the information we receive. It is how we separate surd from substance. Our values are the sieve; they determine what is substance and what is not.

Thinking enables us to make all of life's decisions, and if we have cultivated the right values, we have a greater chance of making the right decisions. Ultimately, the decisions we make determine whether we spend much of our lives looking down from a penthouse or looking up from a state penitentiary.

Our dreams are birthed in our minds.

Our dreams and aspirations are birthed and refined in our minds. Even before we were thought of by our parents, God had already defined a purpose for each of us. When we submit to Him, He will order our thoughts and steps so that we can fully realize that purpose (Psalm 37:23).

The Bible offers additional confirmation in this Scripture: "For it is God who works in you to will and to act according to his good purpose" (Philippians 2:13 NIV). The finest thoughts and ideas that have resulted in great success in our lives were birthed in our hearts by God. Thus, it is incumbent upon us to provide a conducive environment in our hearts so we can hear from God.

Abraham and his nephew Lot are great examples of how our thinking can yield different results. Abraham lived in Bethel and brought his nephew to live with him. They were both prosperous and had large herds of cattle. Before long a quarrel broke out between their herdsmen.

Abraham feared God, and his value system derived from his reverence for Him. Consequently, he sought to quickly resolve the strife. Lot, on the other hand, was a crass materialist. Laws and moral uprightness were irrelevant if they meant passing up an opportunity for immediate aggrandizement.

Pulling Lot aside, Abraham showed him the large expanses of land that surrounded them. He told Lot to choose whichever direction looked best to him. He promised to lead his family in the opposite direction.

Lot had a chance to think through several options. Could his prosperity have been connected to the fact that he lived with Abraham? Could they have found a way to peacefully cohabit? The culture at that period would strongly suggest that Lot should have asked his uncle to make the first choice. Instead, he surveyed the land, looking for water and sumptuous greenery for his flock. He ended up choosing the direction of Sodom and Gomorrah. It looked irresistibly attractive, just like many options that confront us today. If our thought process is defective, we will never see beyond the facade.

Lot headed in his choice direction. Unbeknownst to him, he was heading toward a wicked and perverse people. Not long afterward, a neighboring nation attacked Sodom and captured him and his family. Abraham came to his rescue. Lot could have reconsidered his decision following this captivity, but he chose to return to Sodom.

Soon, the men of Sodom and Gomorrah started to prey on his daughters. Though he was getting a lot more than he had bargained for, he still did not move. God was so dismayed by the sins of these two cities that He decided to destroy them. But Lot had an unrelenting intercessor in Abraham. He went before God and pleaded for deliverance for his nephew. Lot was eventually delivered, but he lost his wife and almost everything he owned because of his self-centered thought process.

Thinking does not produce all the answers.

Thinking, as a process, will not devise all the answers to our questions. After all, faith would be useless if we knew everything and had all the answers we would ever need. The idea is to allow God's Word to order our thinking.

God's Word is light. As we thoughtfully apply it to the innermost recesses of our hearts, it reveals all the dust and cobwebs that need to be cleaned out. Furthermore, it enables us to see whatever is coming into our minds, so we can determine if it will be helpful or hurtful. And it sets us up to clearly see any message or direction that God places in our hearts.

Godly thinking and popular culture.

We cannot be crowd pleasers and concurrently tap into the power that results from meditating on the Word. That is because God's ways are often not the ways of the crowd.

When Moses was leading the people of Israel out of Egypt, they came up against a roadblock. The Egyptian army was behind them, to their sides were mountains, and in front was the Red Sea. Fearing for their lives, the crowd berated Moses. "Why did you bring us out here to die?" they asked. "Were there no graves for us in Egypt?" The crowd looked at their immediate surroundings and concluded that there was no way out.

Sometimes, we find ourselves at a similar juncture. It is up to us to follow the voice of the crowd or turn to our Maker for guidance. God sees beyond our immediate situation. He knows our challenges are temporary, and He sees the light on the horizon. Often, that light is brighter than we ever imagined.

Having experienced God's faithfulness in the past, Moses turned to Him for guidance. When he did, the unprecedented happened! Had he followed the voice of the crowd, the outcome might have been tragically different.

Job presents another worthy example. He was a man who faced grave hardship in his life. The Bible records that he encountered the hardship not because of anything he did wrong (Job 1:1-12). Job was a dedicated servant of God, and the devil thought his dedication stemmed from the abundant blessings God had given him. Little did he know that Job's faith transcended material wealth.

Satan launched a deadly attack on Job and his family. Job lost everything he had and was bedridden with sickness. In that helpless condition, the crowd spoke. It is interesting how the crowd often speaks when you are at your weakest. Just remember that Christ's strength is made perfect in your weakness (2 Corinthians 12:9-10).

Job's wife told him to curse God and die. To her way of thinking, God had abandoned him and his life was a closed chapter. He would be insane to think there was any hope, let alone a bright future for him.

But even in that terrible condition, Job remembered the word of God he had committed to heart, weighed the suggestion in light of the word, and decided not to sin against God. He later received his healing, and the Bible states that he received double of everything he had lost (Job 42:10).

Job's life teaches us that it pays to stick with God!

CHAPTER 6

The Power of Confession

The power of life and death are in the tongue (Proverbs 18:21). The ground we walk on, the clouds above, the plants and animals that surround us, the light we enjoy by day, and the darkness that keeps the night tranquil all came into existence because "God said, Let there be . . . and there was" (Genesis 1:3). The first chapter of Genesis is proof that there is no greater creative power than the power of the tongue. But the tongue serves many other purposes. It can build up or put down, defuse or inflame, possess or lose, bless or curse.

Following God's instruction Moses sent twelve spies to explore Canaan. They were to assess the military might, natural resources, and economic prosperity of Canaan. God wanted to show the people of Israel the bountiful blessings that were in their future so they could be motivated to possess them.

After forty days, the spies returned and confirmed that it was a highly desirable place. They described it as a land that "flows with milk and honey" (Numbers 13:27). But ten of the twelve spies also reported that the city was heavily fortified. They said the strong inhabitants included the Anaks, a tribe of giants.

The other two spies, Caleb and Joshua, saw the situation differently. God had already declared that the land was theirs, and these two men were willing to stand on that promise. They interrupted the defeatist speech of the ten and announced that Israel was able to occupy the land. However, their positive report had no effect on the people as they had already believed the negative confession of the majority of the spies.

So devastating was the pessimistic report that the people bemoaned their fate and accused Moses of deceit and poor judgment. They went a step further to contemplate overthrowing him and appointing a new leader to take them back to captivity. The people of Israel were experiencing the repercussions of making a decision based on a majority opinion as opposed to the will of God. There is nothing inherently wrong with a majority opinion. However, when it contradicts the will of God, God's will should always supercede.

When Joshua and Caleb continued to espouse the belief that Canaan was within their reach, the people threatened to stone them to death (Numbers 14:6-10). They were ready to give up a promising future because they could not confront their fears.

How many times have you given up a great opportunity for fear of opposition? The path to your future is not devoid of opposition. Knowing how to get through is key to your advance.

God was so angry at the unbelief and negativity of Israel that He threatened to destroy them and raise a new nation for Moses to lead (Numbers 14:12). But Moses made a selfless, passionate, and lengthy plea for his followers. He reminded God that Israel's enemies would mock Him if they heard that He had destroyed them. He reminded Him of His patience and great mercy. So persuasive was he that God decided to forgive Israel. Moses' confession defused an otherwise fatal situation. However, the people were not totally exonerated. Due to their unbelief, their generation was barred from entering the Promised Land. But because Joshua and Caleb believed God and confessed faith in His promise, they entered the Land.

Esau and Jacob provide another example of how we can incur irreparable loss by our confession. Esau was a hunter; his brother was described as a quiet man who mostly hung around the house. Their mother, Rebekah, loved Jacob dearly.

One fateful day, Esau came home famished from one of his hunting trips. He returned to the tantalizing aroma of stew that Jacob had made. When he asked to be fed, Jacob promised him all he could eat in exchange for his birthright. How easy it can be to make imprudent compromises in an unguarded moment! Blinded by his hunger, Esau failed to consider the ramifications of his brother's request. He swore to Jacob that he would give up his birthright (Genesis 25:27-34). What he did not immediately realize is that, by his confession, he had given away his God-given position in life for a moment's gratification. It began to dawn on him when Jacob, with their mother's help, robbed him of his father's blessings. He spent a good portion of his adult life regretting his mistake (Genesis 27:1-40).

Salvation comes only by confession.

Confession is how we declare our stand. Faith is belief in the existence of God. But just believing that God exists is not enough. Salvation does not occur until we confess the lordship of Christ. As the Scriptures put it, "For with the heart one believes unto righteousness, and with the mouth confession is made unto salvation" (Romans 10:10).

Apart from not receiving the redemptive power of Christ's death and resurrection, when we fail to confess our belief, people will respond to us on the basis of their own assumptions. If their assumptions are incorrect, we will have to deal with the consequences. Oftentimes, dealing with the consequences means taking a detour from our desired future.

Eschew lies and misleading confessions.

When we intentionally make false or misleading confessions, we set off a chain reaction that will ultimately negate our purpose. Abraham and Sarah faced such a situation. In their travels, they briefly settled in a city called Gerar. Abraham did not know much about the locals, and consequently, he was worried and fearful. He was concerned that they might kill him and take Sarah.

Thus, when Abraham was asked about his relationship with Sarah, he replied that she was his sister. Although it was not a lie since they were somewhat related, he withheld a critical piece of information because of fear (Genesis 20:1-13).

Unaware that they were married, Abimelech, king of Gerar, took Sarah. Had God not intervened, Abraham would have forced adultery on his wife. He could have lost Sarah altogether. Since his blessings were tied to his relationship with Sarah, his losses would have been incalculable.

Nourish your life with godly confessions.

You can choose to call good things into your life. You will have whatever you confess. Jesus invites you to "ask, and it will be given to you" (Matthew 7:7). If you do not know what to ask for, open your Bible and claim the promises that are there. Paul and Peter taught that God is faithful to fulfill all His promises to us (Hebrews 10:23; 2 Peter 3:9). Make a habit of confessing them over your life, family, church, business, and community. There is a promise for every situation. Find the one that's right for your situation and confess it often. Here are some starters:

- If you are unsaved, confess your sins and ask for forgiveness. He promises to forgive all your sins and cleanse you from all unrighteousness (Isaiah 1:18; 1 John 1:9).

- If you are sick, confess that by Christ's stripes you were healed (1 Peter 2:24).

- If you are in need, confess that your God shall supply all your needs according to His riches in glory by Christ Jesus (Philippians 4:19).

- If you are in danger, confess that no weapon formed against you shall prosper and that Christ will be with you always (Isaiah 54:17; Matthew 28:20).

- If you are in need of direction, confess that His word is a lamp unto your feet and a light unto your path, and confess that He will guide you with His eyes and His counsel into the way of peace and into all truth (Psalm 119:105; 32:8; 73:24; Luke 1:79; John 16:13).

- If you feel encircled by the enemy, confess that the Lord is your help and your shield (Psalm 33:20).

- If you are weak, confess that you are strong (Joel 3:10; 2 Corinthians 12:10).

- If you are faced with a difficult task, confess that you can "do all things through Christ who strengthens" you (Philippians 4:13).

- If you need victory, confess that God causes you to triumph always in Christ (2 Corinthians 2:14).

Stick to your confession. God does not take these promises lightly. They are His Word and He regards it very highly (Psalm 138:2). He said that His word will never return to Him void; it must achieve the purpose for which it was spoken (Isaiah 55:11).

Jesus reinforced this declaration by stating that heaven and earth shall pass away, but His word will not (Matthew 24:35). When your actions align with your confessions, God's Word will bear fruit in your life.

Make prayer and praise a part of your daily confession.

Prayer and praise are both integral parts of your confession. You communicate with God through prayer and honor Him by confessing His goodness in praise and worship.

Since the earth is a haven for the devil and legions of other fallen angels, it is full of the trials, temptations, and tribulations that accompany their presence. When these pressures are applied to people's lives, the people seek avenues to vent, let off steam, clear their minds. They often do this by pouring out their concerns to family members, friends, colleagues, psychologists, psychiatrists, or anyone else who will listen. However, the Bible teaches that the most productive way to decompress is by presenting our concerns to God. We are to cast all our cares and burdens on Christ because He cares for us (1 Peter 5:7). We do this through prayer, supplication, and thanksgiving (Philippians 4:6). He promises to hear and answer us when we pray by faith (Matthew 21:22).

Hezekiah, king of Judah, knew how to decompress. In the fourteenth year of his reign, he received a disconcerting letter from Sennacherib, king of Assyria. Sennacherib was a notorious and formidable enemy, and he had threatened in the letter to annex Hezekiah's kingdom.

When Hezekiah received the letter, he did not act the way most of us would: fall apart in tears, throw a pity party, bang our heads against a wall, write a nasty and provocative reply, run out of town, or mail the letter to friends so they can join forces with us. Instead, he took the letter to the house of God and spread it out before Him (2 Kings 19:14). He was in tune with the source of his strength. He knew that Sennacherib's long history of oppression was no match for the power of God.

He prayed to God for help and guidance. Sennacherib's army never made it into Judah because God took care of the situation without Hezekiah or his people shooting a single arrow!

Praise and prayer will open any doors the enemy has shut. The enemy had free access to your life before you accepted Christ. During that time, he could have led you in a direction that shut you out of important blessings and opportunities. But now that you are saved, you can turn to God to open any shut door to your progress. Rest assured that if He opens a door, no one can shut it (Revelation 3:8).

When Paul and Silas were thrown into prison, they raised their voices in praise and prayer. They were in jail because the enemy wanted to intercept the spreading of the gospel that was occurring all too rapidly under Paul's leadership.

But they were prepared for every eventuality. They knew their God would deliver them and therefore wholeheartedly called on Him. God heard their voices and responded in a great earthquake that threw the prison doors open (Acts 16:16-40).

When Joshua was poised to take Jericho, God commanded his army to walk around the city walls once a day for six days, and on the seventh day, to walk around the city seven times, then raise their voices in praise. When they did as God directed, His power came down and the walls crumbled (Joshua 6:1-27).

Praise is a powerful way to bring God into your situation. The Bible states that He inhabits the praises of His people (Psalm 22:3). If you want to see Him move powerfully in your situation, give Him praise!

Eschew cursing.

James warns that blessing and cursing should not proceed from the same mouth (James 3:10). It is hypocritical to expect God to accept your praise when you have been defiled by your tongue.

No matter how provocative a situation might be, it is better not to utter a word than to sputter a curse. Though it may provide immediate gratification to a vengeful urge, cursing defiles us, dishonors God, and contradicts His Word. As Christ put it, it is not what goes into a man that defiles him, but what comes out of him (Matthew 15:11). He further pointed out that anyone who curses shall be "in danger of hell fire" (Matthew 5:22).

Christ requires us to bless those who curse us (Matthew 5:44). Admittedly, it is hard to sincerely speak blessings over people who wish us ill. But His grace is sufficient for us. If we ask Him, He will enable us to live up to His Word. That way, we will never have occasion to undercut the blessings that attend our confessions.

You fight and win spiritual battles with your confessions.

The Word is the sword of the Spirit and confession is how we wield it. You need to confess the Word to break free if you are bound in an area of your life (you have difficulty prospering in that area), if you are under a curse, if you have an enduring weakness in your walk with the Lord, if you need healing, if you need deliverance, if you need a miracle, or if you need any other kind of divine intervention.

Confession is how you change the course of your life. If there is anything that is not in line with your intended future, reject it, and by faith, claim the future God has prepared for you. Your salvation is a testimony to Christ's saving grace. Share it, along with everything else He has done for you. It is how you overcome (Revelation 12:11).

Mobilize others to good work with your confession.

Confession is your tool for stirring up faith in others and mobilizing them for action. At the edge of the Red Sea, when the people of Israel were stuck between a rock and a hard place, Moses ratcheted up his faith and made this famous statement: "Do not be afraid. Stand still, and see the salvation of the Lord, which He will accomplish for you today. For the Egyptians whom you see today, you shall see again no more forever. The Lord will fight for you, and you shall hold your peace" (Exodus 14:13-14). That statement quieted the rambunctious crowd.

In another moment of truth, Joshua gave a stomp speech at Shechem to a people who were compromising their faith by indulging in idolatry. It was his last speech as leader and he needed to reestablish the place of Jehovah God in Israel. He said, "Now therefore, fear the Lord, serve Him in sincerity and in truth, and put away the gods which your fathers served on the other side of the River and in Egypt. Serve the Lord! And if it seems evil to you to serve the Lord, choose for yourselves this day whom you will serve. . . . But as for me and my house, we will serve the Lord" (Joshua 24:14-15). After that speech, the offenders destroyed the strange gods, and all of Israel declared with one voice that they would serve the Lord.

Practice using your confession to encourage people to make the right choices and move in the right direction. Doing this can only enhance your success.

Make thanksgiving part of your daily confession.

Learn to be thankful. God resents ingratitude. Always approach His throne with thanksgiving. As David put it, "Enter into His gates with thanksgiving, and into His courts with praise. Be thankful to Him, and bless His name" (Psalm 100:4).

If you are not sure what to be thankful for, listen to the evening news or visit your local hospital or morgue or police department or courthouse or prison. You will find several reasons to give thanks.

Ten lepers approached Jesus in tears on His way to Jerusalem.

They cried out to Him to heal them. Moved with compassion, Jesus instructed them to go show themselves to the priests. These men wanted the Messiah to heal them, not to send them to the priests they probably saw often. They could have argued the directive or simply ignored Him. But their miracle was in their obedience. When they did as He commanded, they were healed along the way.

When one of them noticed he was healed, he turned around to see Jesus, and the Bible records that with a loud voice, he thanked and glorified God. Jesus then asked him a rhetorical question. He had healed ten people but only one came back. Where were the nine? I'm sure God is asking the same question of most of us today. Christ blessed the man before releasing him. Those other nine missed out on this blessing (Luke 17:11-19).

An attitude of gratitude costs nothing to acquire and yields amazing returns. It is human nature to be appreciated, and a simple "thank you" can cause a friend or coworker to go the extra mile. As people who seek to model excellence, just saying "thank you" does not suffice for every situation. Sometimes, you might need to tax your brain, or your wallet, to produce something unique and indelible.

Consider these modified versions of thank-you notes that I have written to friends. The first was a letter to a supportive and caring manager. The second was an ode to a supervisor for a successful year at work.

> Dear ...,
>
> One of the daunting ironies of the written word is that it barely suffices as a medium for describing the spectacular. Perhaps it's not meant to.
>
> I suppose pictures exist to fill that vacuum. As we unwittingly cascade down the cataract of eternity, they crystallize and perpetualize our fleeting but extraordinary moments.
>
> The enclosed picture is a token of my appreciation for the unmatched support you've given me in my first year with this organization. Your selfless commitment to the betterment of others will never go unnoticed.

Remember always that:
The daily kindness you show,
Great or small it may be,
Is a silver lining that glows
In the clouded minds of budding leaders.

Ode to Jim

Only the trumpet and the flute
That made Solomon's temple
A paradise on earth
Can express in clearer terms
Your noble leadership role in life.
Let the string instruments resound
And the percussionists revel
In the art they most excel
On the hill where we crown
Jim A.
Leader of the Year!

Needless to say, these notes injected a significant dose of good-will in my relationships with these individuals.

The more faces you can light up with your gratitude, the brighter the path to your future will be.

Important reminder.

Remember, "out of the abundance of the heart the mouth speaks" (Matthew 12:34). The Word of God has to be in you for you to be able to recall and confess it. Load up on it!

Unlike the secularized quotes peddled by many motivational speakers, there is undying power in the Word. Let it work for you!

CHAPTER 7

Walking by Faith

Your future is a call to action, and acting by faith is how to respond.

Faith is your key to unlimited possibilities. While great ideas are birthed through the thought process, they are articulated in words as a vision. The effort involved in actualizing the vision is referred to as "faith walking," "walk of faith," or "walking by faith."

Many a dream appears unrealistic at the outset. Critical resources may not be available, and the outcome of the dream may be contingent upon an entity over which you have no control. Yet you are convinced it came from God, and you have refined and nurtured it so much that there is no trace of doubt in your mind about its achievability. You realize you cannot achieve the dream on your own and believe that the path to the desired outcome entails complete dependence on God. Since He always honors faith, doors open for you as you forge ahead in this mind-set. (See Matthew 9:22, 29; Luke 7:50.) This is how we have been called to live.

The Bible declares that "faith by itself, if it does not have works, is dead" (James 2:17). The world is awash with unfulfilled dreams. There is never a dearth of talk about what could have, should have, or would have been. However, very few people dare to go out on a limb in pursuit of their dreams. And among those few, many surrender at the feet of obstacles.

Famed as the wisest man who ever lived, Solomon wrote that it is foolish to trust in one's heart (Proverbs 28:26). Put differently, it is unwise to rely on your limited abilities in confronting your future. Activate your faith and give God room to operate on your behalf. You activate faith by taking steps to actualize your dream regardless of what your current reality dictates. In so doing, you will be demonstrating to God that you trust Him with your future. He will not disappoint you (Hebrews 13:5).

Walking by faith means putting God first.

If you earnestly desire the extraordinary results that God gives, He has to be first in your life. God does not play second fiddle to anyone or anything. He etched in stone the fact that we cannot have any other god besides Him (Exodus 20:3).

However, it is a human tendency to only want the benefits God gives and ignore the rest of His Word. Ahab strongly exhibited that tendency. He was a king who worshiped a foreign god, perverted justice, and murdered the innocent. Yet each time he was confronted with a war, he summoned the prophets of God to find out if he should go or not. In the last war he fought, about four hundred of his prophets prophesied victory. These prophets saw victory because God had allowed a lying spirit to come upon them. When Micaiah, a prophet of God, prophesied that he would be killed, Ahab threw him in jail. Ahab died in the battle (1 Kings 22:1-28).

As the Scriptures rightfully note, God cannot be mocked. Whatever we sow is what we will reap (Galatians 6:7).

Jesus advised us to seek first the kingdom of God and His righteousness. Thereafter, *everything else* shall be added (Matthew 6:33). God cannot give a future that leads you away from Him. No matter how famous, powerful, or wealthy you may be, if you are engaged in an activity that undermines Him, you are operating outside His will for your life, and you need to retrace your steps.

You may achieve fame, power, and wealth as you live out your destiny, but they are not proof that you are progressing toward your intended future. By all worldly standards, Paul was a successful lawyer and statesman before he was converted. But he was not, by any stretch of the imagination, fulfilling the future God intended for him. If anything, his pre-conversion legacy included extensive efforts to limit the spread of the gospel. It was not until after his salvation that he began to experience the divine purpose for his life.

A rich young man once asked Jesus what he needed to do to have eternal life. Jesus initially replied by asking him about portions of the Ten Commandments. His response was that he had kept them from when he was a child (Mark 10:19-20). Despite the fact that this young man kept a tradition of observing the commandments, he still felt that something was missing.

Many people religiously maintain a prayer or church attendance routine. They do so not because they are seeking the kingdom of God or His righteousness, but because it is a tradition they have become accustomed to. However, such acts do not translate to putting God first. True worshipers must be willing and ready to demonstrate their faithfulness by surrendering anything that can get in the way of their relationship with God. In the above example, Christ asked the young man to sell all he had and follow Him. But he walked away distressed because he was very rich (vs. 21-22). His riches came between him and God.

Faith comes from hearing the Word.

Just as the human body cannot survive without nourishment, your faith will die without spiritual food. The Word creates and grows faith in you (Romans 10:17). Therefore it is critical to always immerse yourself in it.

In addition to self-study, find a Bible-believing church where you will be taught the ways of God. God promises to provide pastors who will increase your knowledge and understanding of His Word (Jeremiah 3:15). All around us, evidence abounds that He is fulfilling that promise.

You can also gain understanding by interacting with other believers. As the Bible puts it, "Iron sharpens iron" (Proverbs 27:17 NIV). By rubbing minds with people who have developed their knowledge of the Word, everyone attains a higher level of understanding. Thus, your attitude toward being in the house of God should be joyful. The psalmist set a great example: "I was glad when they said to me, 'Let us go into the house of the Lord' " (Psalm 122:1).

Faith walking means living by the Word.

Faith is not a marriage of convenience between the world and the Word. If we profess it, we must walk in absolute obedience to God. This is pivotal to maintaining our relationship with Him.

Noah lived in obedience, and as a result, he and his family were the only people who survived the flood. Abraham was so faithful that he was willing to sacrifice his only son to God. Joseph demonstrated faithfulness when he was tempted by Potiphar's wife. He was also exemplary in prison and continued to obey God after he was promoted to a leadership position in Egypt. Moses took a stand for God when he gave up Pharaoh's riches in favor of the God of his fathers. And Elijah was so faithful that he did not die (2 Kings 2:11). Their examples are proof that we too can walk in obedience.

We model our faith by our lifestyle before a curious world. We may not all be able to stand behind a pulpit every Sunday, but we can let our families, friends, and associates in on the Word by the way we conduct our lives. Paul admonished believers to exemplify our faith in speech, life, love, faith, and purity (1 Timothy 4:12).

Through faith modeling Shadrach, Meshach, Abednego, and Daniel caused two kings to recognize and worship the God of Israel. You have the grace to follow in their footsteps.

Walking by faith does not mean we are perfect.

Temptation will come, and sometimes we will make mistakes. What matters is how we respond after we realize our mistake. First John 2:1 tells us that the Word of God can keep us from sinning. However, if we fall into sin, we have an advocate with the Father, the Lord Jesus Christ, who intercedes for us. When we reach out for help, His hands will be there to uphold us. "The steps of a good man," writes the psalmist, "are ordered by the Lord, and He delights in his way. Though he fall, he shall not be utterly cast down; for the Lord upholds him with His hand" (Psalm 37:23). Proverbs 24:16 reinforces this point by stating that even if the righteous fall seven times, they will rise again. The prophet Micah advised his enemies not to celebrate when he fell because he would certainly rise again (Micah 7:8).

James describes the proper attitude when we are experiencing a temptation. He instructs us to consider it "pure joy" (a positive experience), because in trying our faith, it produces patience. He adds that patience must work on us so we can mature and be complete (James 1:2-4 NIV).

James taught us that there is a lesson in every temptation, and we would be foolish to ignore it. The sooner we approach trials and temptations with the right attitude, the quicker our redemption will come. Psalm 34:19 remarks, "Many are the afflictions of the righteous, but the Lord delivers him out of them all." No matter what temptation we fall into, if we dust ourselves off and get back on track, God will lead us to our desired future.

Concentrate on doing good.

Faith walking demands that we do the right thing in every situation. Faith does not cut corners. It is not self-serving. Jesus went about doing good throughout His earthly ministry. He welcomed everyone, children and grown-ups, men and women, rich and poor, into His presence. Salvation is the greatest good that humanity can have and He delivered His message at every opportunity He got. When He kept the people too long, He fed them. When they had occasion to celebrate, He joined in. When they mourned, He shared their grief. He healed the sick and raised the dead among them. Everyone could tell that He had been someplace by the testimonies that followed.

Jesus' faithfulness, kindness, and fairness were not limited to His family and allies. He did not do the right thing only when it worked in His favor. Although He knew Judas was going to betray him, He had dinner with him and washed his feet afterward. After He had been severely beaten and nailed to the cross, He prayed for God to forgive His torturers. He exemplified His instruction to us to pray for our enemies and do good to those who hate us (Matthew 5:44). We therefore have no excuse to act differently if we find ourselves in similar situations.

God gives us the capability to do good. Paul wrote, "God is able to make all grace abound to you, so that in all things at all times, having all that you need, you will abound in every good work" (2 Corinthians 9:8 NIV). So if you feel ill-equipped to please God in every situation, ask for His grace.

When we choose to do good by faith—that is, when we stretch our abilities or resources in order to do the right thing—God multiplies our blessings. When the widow of Zarephath gave her family's last meal to Elijah, she was "stretching" to do the right thing. As a result, she and her son did not run out of food throughout an extended drought (1 Kings 17:8-16).

You are walking either by faith or by sight.

The Bible teaches that we should walk by faith, not by sight (2 Corinthians 5:7). Walking by sight is like being lost in a dark and convoluted forest without a flashlight. Sometimes you trip. Other times you fall. The uncertainty of the terrain prohibits you from proceeding speedily or steadily. When you think you are gaining proficiency, you discover you are only meandering in a circle. Throughout the journey, fear of succumbing to hunger, getting injured, wild animals, careless or malicious hunters, and dying alone gets the best of you. Sometimes, you wonder how you got there. Often, you doubt you will make it. But somehow you find the courage to trudge along. Over time, you begin to acclimate to the environment; darkness becomes acceptable, and walking into dead ends is rationalized as a way of life. A journey that should have taken ten days takes ten years. In the end, you console yourself by believing that you did your best. But you know, deep in your heart, it was not good enough.

After they left Egypt, the Israelites walked by sight, not by faith. Though they saw God in action as He coerced a recalcitrant Pharaoh into freeing them and made a path through the Red Sea, they did not trust that He had a good plan for them. The fact that He sent them quail and manna from heaven, and supplied them water from a rock, did not change their minds. Their modus operandi was to fret and complain every time they faced a challenge. The last straw was when they rejected the Promised Land. God was so disappointed He cursed them. For every one of the forty days the spies spent exploring the land, they would spend a year in the wilderness. And all the men who did not believe they could possess the land would die in the desert during those forty years. Such is the consequence of faithlessness (Exodus 5-10; Numbers 14:1-45).

It takes faith to finish.

Just as it requires faith to launch your vision, it takes faith to achieve all that God intends for you. Achieving your future is like running a long-distance race; remembering everything you have learned about running skillfully, keeping your goal in sight, and having strong faith that you will achieve it all help to build and sustain endurance throughout the race.

At the end of his ministry, Paul cheerfully pronounced that he had "finished the race" and was ready for his reward (2 Timothy 4:7). His attitude toward the ministry accounted for his success. Even after the Holy Spirit revealed to him that he would be bound and afflicted in Jerusalem, he still embarked on the journey. In his words, "None of these things move me; nor do I count my life dear to myself, so that I may finish my race with joy, and the ministry which I received from the Lord Jesus, to testify to the gospel of the grace of God" (Acts 20:24). This Scripture is evidence that he put God first in all he did. When you put God first, He will be there for you.

Peter demonstrated how we can start by faith and falter along the way. He and the other disciples were out in the sea on a particularly turbulent night. Having left them to pray in the mountains, Jesus started to make His way back to the ship by walking on the sea. When they saw Him, fear gripped their hearts. Their fearfulness is reminiscent of our reaction when we are focusing on our problems. We tend to miss the answer in front of us. Even after Christ announced that it was Him, they were still fussing and screaming.

Inspired by the miracle he was witnessing, Peter asked Jesus to invite him to join in the faith walk. Jesus acquiesced, and onto the water Peter jumped. Like Christ, Peter walked on water. For a moment, he defied the law of gravity and had the time of his life!

But Peter began to lose his focus on Christ. He noticed the bois-terous wind—the challenges in his path—and that put doubt in him. Right away, he began to sink. But before he drowned, he called out for help and Jesus rescued him (Matthew 14:22-33).

Our ability to complete whatever we start is proportional to our degree of focus. When we start to lose sight of what counts, we begin to lay the foundation for failure. If you find yourself in such a situation, trace back your steps to when you started to drift and do what you should have done in the first place. If you are in a desperate situation, as Peter was, do not drown in silence; fall on your knees and call on the Lord for help. You will be amazed at how close He is and how quickly and powerfully He will respond.

Faith walking and human experiences.

There is a didactic essence to every human experience. Find out what your experiences are supposed to be teaching you. They can be excellent pointers in your journey. However, lessons from experience can be a two-edged sword. The fact that they can alter your thinking and values, and consequently shape future action, presents a dilemma.

When people get burned, they tend to avoid fires. But the path to their future may very well run through a fire. They must not forget that fire can serve different purposes: it can consume or refine. If they see themselves as dry leaves, they will be devoured. If, on the other hand, they perceive themselves as gold, fire will unleash their hidden beauty. There is a hidden talent in every one of us. If we walk by faith, every experience will reveal and strengthen it.

Shadrach, Meshach, and Abednego were willing to be thrown into a furnace to defend their faith. They believed that God would deliver them, and even if He did not, that was not going to change their resolve about experiencing the furnace because it was the right thing to do. Their unwavering faith brought them honor, fame, promotion, and freedom. Better yet, an entire nation recognized the true God because of their courageous stand.

Whereas the experience of the Hebrew trio resulted from obedience, Jonah had a sweltering experience in the belly of a fish due to his disobedience. This prophet wanted to control where he delivered God's message. Consequently, he was swallowed by a fish. For three days, he lived in a dark, putrid, mucus-infested solitary confinement. He was deprived of food, water, family, friends, and a bath! Power, money, and all the pleasures of life did not mean a thing at this point. He was lost in a fish in the middle of an ocean!

Jonah had a lot of thinking time, and by the third day, he had come to the right conclusion. Thereafter, the fish coughed him up, and in no time he was delivering God's message in the right place (Jonah 1:1-17; 2:1-2; 3:1-4).

The most important take-away from Jonah's ordeal is that the harrowing experience he endured could have been avoided. As we often do, he created pain and agony for himself by going against God's will.

Moses exemplified how an experience can produce undesired consequences. He had a difficult time leading a people who complained often, challenged his leadership, and sometimes threatened his life. Though he was very patient, the cumulative effect of those difficulties took a toll on him. Consequently, he made a mistake that prevented him from entering Canaan.

Samson presents another important scenario of how our experiences can yield unintended results. He was a superhuman Nazarite (consecrated to God) whose physical strength was intended to deliver Israel from the Philistines.

However, Samson had a problem with lust. Having felt no danger from a number of previous affairs, he continued until he met Delilah, a woman from the enemy camp. He frequented her house, and in the process, began to let his guard down in the enemy territory. The erotic bliss wore on him so much he ignored all warnings. Following repeated requests from Delilah, he disclosed the secret to his success, and minutes later, the Philistines plucked out his eyes. Then they threw him in jail, hoping to sacrifice him to Dagon, their idol. Although Dagon did not have that pleasure, Samson died along with many Philistines because of his carelessness (Judges 14-16:1-31).

Samson's example teaches us that even after we have become successful, we still need to walk by faith. If anything, we should be closer to God than ever. It is better to experience setbacks in the preparatory phase of our lives than to collapse from the pinnacle of our vision.

Character Development

CHAPTER 8

Unchanging Truth

Change is an inescapable feature of human existence. Children change into adults, parents into grandparents, grandparents into great-grandparents, and so on. Similarly, weak and dysfunctional organizations seek to become nimble and high performing; underdeveloped nations would like nothing more than to achieve socio-economic prosperity. Change is the only means by which we, and the institutions we construct, transition from one state of being to another. It is the process by which we achieve our full potential.

In the midst of a changing world, however, is an everlasting constant: truth. It is not subject to the law of change. The Bible states it lives forever and is the same to all generations (Psalm 117:2; 100:5). And contrary to certain contemporary notions, it is not relative.

Perhaps the most destructive of these notions is moral relativism. Essentially, this theory portends that there is an acceptable middle ground between truth and lies. Moral relativists insist that the world is better off in this middle territory. Their contribution to the deepening degeneracy of society is not insignificant. The legalization of abortion, ongoing movements to legalize same-sex marriage, efforts to eliminate God and prayer from public schools, and the ordination of gay priests, to mention a few, draw impetus from their ideology. They will continue to gain ground unless godly men and women rise up to defend truth.

What is truth?

There is only one truth. David tells us that God's law is truth (Psalm 119:142). All of His commands are truth (vs. 151). The Word in its entirety is truth (John 17:17; 2 Timothy 2:15).

Christ is the personification of the Word; he is, therefore, truth (Matthew 5:17; John 1:1-14; 14:6). If you know Him, you know truth.

God demands that we worship Him in spirit and in truth (John 4:24). The Bible adds that He desires "truth in the inward parts" (Psalm 51:6). This means that truth, or the Word, must be the basis of all our thoughts, decisions, and actions. Truth must be the core of our character. We must seek, stand on, act on, and defend truth at all times (Ephesians 4:25). If we miss the centrality of truth in our character-building effort, all other desirable character traits that we develop will be flawed.

The nature of truth.

There are three significant spiritual ramifications to truth.

a. *Truth is indestructible.* As the Latin maxim goes, *vincit omnia veritas*—truth conquers all things. Paul wrote that we can do nothing against truth (2 Corinthians 13:8). Even if we tried, it would always surface, and whether in this life or in the life after, it will always prevail.

Some of the leaders in Christ's day fomented a lie to suppress His resurrection. They posited that His disciples had stolen His body while the guards were asleep. Little did they know that Christ had a plan to reveal His glorious post-resurrection body to a coterie of witnesses. They were also ignorant of the power of His resurrection.

Thus, it was to their chagrin that the disciples had great success in spreading the word. The more these political and religious leaders tried to suppress them, the more successful they became. Such is the potency of truth; it will germinate wherever it lands.

Similar to Christ's and His disciples' experience, those who proclaim and defend truth will encounter opposition. They will be treated unjustly and will often be in the minority (Matthew 5:11-12; 10:22). From the beginning, Satan has been on a mission to distort truth, and he will not stop with our generation.

Nevertheless, we must not be dismayed or threatened by the badgering of the enemy. We maintain our focus, confidence, and joy by saturating our hearts with the Word and making it the driver of our daily activities. We preserve our victory by resisting the devil in all his manifestations. His only option then is to flee (James 4:7). He runs because he is a defeated foe (Luke 10:18; Revelation 1:18; John 16:33).

b. *Truth assures peace.* In Philippians 4:7, Paul prayed that the peace of God, which exceeds all human understanding, would always keep our hearts and minds through Jesus Christ.

The peace that Paul prayed for originates from the Greek word *eirene*. It refers to mental and emotional prosperity. It is a continuous state of psychological wholeness and tranquility that results from a harmonious relationship with God through Jesus Christ. It is the highest and most desired level of well-being.

Money, power, fame, and all other forms of earthly prosperity cannot give this peace. If unsaved people of means would be brutally honest, they will admit that they hardly ever experience this kind of peace. Deep down in their hearts, they recognize that there is more to life than an insatiable quest for self-gratification. They worry about the unknown, about death and life after death, about God's existence, about someday accounting for what they did with their lives, and about heaven and hell. Some of these concerns drove Zacchaeus, a wealthy tax official, to abandon his ways and seek Christ (Luke 19:2).

Those tormented by a guilty conscience, and those who knowingly commit acts of wickedness, cannot experience God's peace (Isaiah 48:22; 57:21). They are tortured by concerns about their safety and security. They constantly look over their shoulders and sit up in the dead of night, wondering when their sins will catch up with them. Paranoia takes the place of peace in their lives. Sadly, they have a valid reason to be worried, as the Scriptures declare that the wicked will not go unpunished (Proverbs 11:21).

The only way to experience real peace is by believing and

operating in the truth. The Bible says that Jesus is our peace (Ephesians 2:14), and He has freely and unreservedly offered Himself (John 14:27). It is up to us to reach out and accept Him. After we have accepted Him, we must allow the peace that He offers to guard our hearts. It must override every thought that puts us in a state of unrest, worry, or anxiety. We must allow it to flow through us into our relationship with others. The Scriptures require that we do so (1 Thessalonians 5:13; Hebrews 12:14).

c. *Real freedom comes from truth.* In Christ's words, "You shall know the truth, and the truth shall make you free" (John 8:32). Christ was speaking of the most important kind of freedom: spiritual freedom. It is a freedom that wealth, cultural heritage, and political systems cannot offer. Religiosity does not provide it either. It comes only from being liberated from the bondage of sin and death.

With salvation comes an ushering into a realm where we are able to operate as God intended us to. Never again would we worry about the curse of sin or the machination and oppression of the enemy. In Christ's words, "If the Son therefore shall make you free, you shall be free indeed" (John 8:36 KJV). As in the days of the early apostles, the greater the opposition, the bolder we will become and the more dynamically we will deliver the message of Christ. Boldness in the face of obstacles is characteristic of a truth-based life.

Freedom has a price, and spiritual freedom costs more than anyone could afford. It cost the life of the only begotten Son of God, and that payment cannot be made twice. If we take Christ's shed blood for granted, we will be denying ourselves the only opportunity not only to enjoy the fullness of God's blessings on earth, but to avoid eternal damnation.

Those who have experienced real freedom do not keep mute; they passionately share their freedom with others. Matthew tells the story of two men whom Christ freed from physical blindness. After their healing, Jesus adjured them not to tell anyone of their experience as it was not time for Him to be revealed. But no sooner had they left His presence than they began to spread the word (Matthew 9:27-31; 12:16-21).

Such is the excitement that true freedom brings. It is abnormal that those who have experienced it would try to conceal it. Besides,

Christ commanded us to share the message of freedom with as many people as would listen. Their future depends on our obedience.

Truth, justice, and equity.

Justice and equity (or fairness) are of utmost importance to God. They form the basis of interaction in heaven (Psalm 89:14). He requires His children to cultivate them and demands that they guide relationships on earth. They are to constitute the basis of our value system (Micah 6:8; Isaiah 33:5).

Justice refers to the ability to correctly interpret rules, to discern right from wrong, and to impartially assign punishment and reward. Equity is the ability to consistently apply justice and to consistently treat people right.

These two concepts cannot operate without rules. God set a rule for Adam and Eve in the garden. He wrote the Ten Commandments for Israel and inspired several people to pen the Bible for our benefit.

God's rules or laws stem from truth. It therefore follows that we cannot do justice or treat people fairly if we lack knowledge of truth. If the laws from which justice is administered are flawed, justice cannot prevail. The law that legitimizes abortion in the United States is a prime example. Regardless of the intent of its writers, the injustice in murdering an innocent child cannot be overstated.

Furthermore, justice cannot prevail if the people charged with administering it lack wisdom or are prejudicial. It was such injustice that nailed Christ to the cross and resulted in the martyrdom of several of His followers. Lamenting a situation in which truth was suppressed, Isaiah wrote, "Truth is fallen in the street, and equity cannot enter" (Isaiah 59:14). The entire book of Proverbs was written to teach us wisdom, justice, and equity (Proverbs 1:2-3). It is prudent for us to study it carefully.

God abhors injustice. To do justice is more acceptable to Him than sacrifices (Proverbs 21:3). He commands us to keep justice (Isaiah 56:1). We are to defend the poor, afflicted, widow, fatherless, and orphan (Psalm 82:3; 140:12). We are to always act justly, even when the parties involved are incapable of challenging us if we did otherwise.

God keeps account of how we apply justice and equity, and He will judge us accordingly. Being the judge of all, He will reward us if we treat others fairly and equitably. He will mete out punishment for unjust decisions and actions. As the Word puts it, we will reap what we sow (Galatians 6:7).

CHAPTER 9

Preparation

God's plan for your life entails a series of progressive assign- ments. You will have to prove your faithfulness in small assignments before you can move on to bigger and better ones (Luke 16:10; Matthew 25:23). Proper and adequate preparation is key to successfully completing any assignment. The more prepared you are, the easier it will be to progress from one level of responsi- bility to another.

Conversely, if you have a laissez-faire attitude toward prepara- tion, not only will your progress be sluggish, you might never achieve your full potential. It is imperative to study, understand, and apply the six tenets of preparation identified below.

Tenet 1: Create a life of discipline.

Discipline is the restraint that prevents our will or freedom of choice from destroying us. It is the willingness to create and the ability to conform to a plan of action. It overrides personal weak- ness, self-indulgence, laziness, wanton desire, hopelessness, and any other excuse to consistently achieve a desired result. It maxi- mizes efficiency in that things are always done at set times. A disciplined person is credible and trustworthy, as his words always match his actions. Without discipline, none of the other tenets listed below will work.

God has called us to live a life of discipline. Just as we cannot please Him without faith, it is impossible to serve Him faithfully with a carefree lifestyle. We can neither reliably endure persecution nor consistently fend off temptation if we lack discipline. The devil is masterful at locking on to areas of inconsistency in our lives, and no matter how hard we strive to break free, we will not succeed until we habitualize the proper response.

The Scriptures clearly show that those who successfully served God in biblical epochs were highly disciplined people. Job was able to overcome the enormous difficulties he faced because he had disciplined his mind to trust God in every situation. Even after he lost everything and everyone that mattered to him and was hanging on to life by the skin of his teeth, he said of God, "Though he slay me, yet will I trust Him" (Job 13:15). Job's faith lingered because long before his troubles, he had taught himself to consistently rely on God. Discipline will keep you from wavering in times of trial and enable you to attain heights that you would otherwise not reach.

Daniel also led a disciplined life. The Bible describes him as a man who had no fault in him (Daniel 6:4). He was highly favored of God and loved by the kings he served. Everything he touched prospered greatly (Daniel 6:3).

Daniel's remarkable success stemmed from his close relationship with God as borne out by his faultless faith walk and consistent prayer life. The Bible records that he consistently prayed three times every day (Daniel 6:10). He was so used to it that even when his life was threatened, he did not miss a beat.

David taught himself to pray three times daily (Psalm 55:17). Though he encountered many enemies throughout his life, his prayers were not in vain, as he always came out victorious.

Daniel and David teach us that a strong prayer life is crucial to achieving all that God has destined for us. Paul drives home the point by admonishing us to "pray without ceasing" (1 Thessalonians 5:17). Since God is the most knowledgeable authority on our future, it makes sense that we would want to be close to Him.

Joshua's life further demonstrates the role of discipline in attempting to achieve one's destiny. God told Joshua that the only way he would be successful was to study and meditate on His laws day and night—birthdays, "bad" days, weekends, and holidays included! He further instructed Joshua to allow the laws to guide his steps (Joshua 1:7-8).

Two important lessons are inherent in these instructions. First, God taught Joshua how to cultivate discipline. It only comes from rigorous practice. We must subject our unwieldy selves to constant study and meditation of the Word. That is the only way we can get it to take root in us. Second, we must make a decision to consistently practice what we read. Some of us have mastered the habit of hearing, reading, or saying one thing and doing another. It is a spiritual malady, and we need to pray for the grace to overcome it.

Discipline applies to both mind and body. Our eating habits, for instance, are a simple test of our degree of self-discipline. If you find yourself going back time and again to food you had vowed never to put in your body, chances are that the same laxity exists in other areas of your life. A structured, determined, repeated, and prayer-backed effort is required to quash any undesired habit.

Tenet 2: Study as much as you can whenever you can.

My vice principal in high school had a favorite saying: "No knowledge is lost." Indeed, everything we learn, good or bad, impacts our thoughts and actions. This is why Scripture instructs us on what to learn. We are to learn to fear God (Deuteronomy 31:13), learn the Word (Romans 15:4), and learn wisdom (Proverbs 19:8). Everything else we learn should be based on this tripartite foundation. This will prevent us from being misled.

The Bible requires that we be ready at all times to discuss our faith. This means that we should familiarize ourselves with the Word so much that we can comfortably and properly apply it to any topic of discussion at any time. We will be doing ourselves and the entire body of Christ a disservice if we cannot confidently present the message of Christ when the opportunity arises.

Building on the above-mentioned foundation makes us wiser than the enemy (Psalm 119:98). No longer do we fret from his threat because we understand that all his plots against us will come to naught.

The Word enables us to attain a higher level of understanding than our teachers (Psalm 119:99). This is primarily because of the indwelling Holy Spirit who, as we study and meditate on the Scriptures, gives us insight into the secret things of God. Contrary to popular opinion, experience is not the best teacher; the Holy Spirit is. The Bible says that He will teach us all things (John 14:26). Believers who are filled with the Holy Ghost should therefore be among the brightest people on earth. The world should be able to easily tell the difference in abilities between us and an unsaved acquaintance, classmate, or colleague. If this power is not working for you, pray for the infilling of the Holy Spirit. Your life will never be the same!

Formal education, self-study, seminars, conferences, workshops, etc. are some of the opportunities we can avail ourselves of in preparing for our desired future. Your talent will take you places, but not before it has been discovered and refined. To discover your talent, study as voraciously as you can, and maximize any opportunity you get to apply what you have learned. From this perspective, work is not the strenuous chore that people dread to take on, but an exciting opportunity to discover, develop, and invest the treasures God has placed in you.

Educational systems throughout the world provide an opportunity to systematically acquire knowledge, and people interested in achieving their full potential should take advantage of them. In fact, increasing learning is a goal that Scripture espouses (Proverbs 1:5). Not only will it enhance your ability to communicate the Word authoritatively, you will be more effective at applying the Christocentric framework in scrutinizing secular knowledge.

For Christians, a significant part of our learning process involves unlearning the world culture. Our culture of sin pervades all aspects of our existence. So entrenched is it that believers sometimes have difficulty deciphering what is right and acceptable to the Lord. It therefore behooves us to constantly examine our lives to ensure that no area is inadvertently captive to the world.

Studying is laborious and expensive. Even elementary education can cost thousands of dollars. However, be reminded that every good and perfect gift comes from God. If you lack the means to provide a good education for yourself or loved ones, go before Him in prayer. He has promised to supply your needs. Besides, ignorance can be more expensive. It ultimately leads to destruction (Hosea 4:6).

Tenet 3: Strive for excellence.

Excellence is striving to be the best that you can be. It is different from striving to be right at all times, or constantly competing with others to surpass them. Instead of laboring to become what you were not created to be, it is a sincere desire and effort to utilize your talent to the fullest. It demands that you avail yourself of every opportunity to sharpen existing skills or acquire new ones. It further requires a desire to experiment with new ideas. Thus, excellence-minded people are not averse to change. If anything, they see it as a platform to test and further develop their talents.

Furthermore, excellence is trusting God with our resources and circumstances. Putting our trust in God causes divine excellence to work in our behalf. The Bible states that on our own, "we can do nothing" (John 15:5). It then adds that "we can do all things through Christ who strengthens" us (Philippians 4:13).

The story of the prophet's wife whose husband left behind a significant debt is a clear demonstration of divine excellence. When his creditors learned of his death, they threatened to take his two sons as slaves if his wife could not pay the debt. She made a decision that turned her family's situation around for good. Instead of panicking, hiding the children, working two or more jobs, or simply surrendering to the situation, she took her concerns to God through Elisha, the prophet her husband had served. Evidently, she realized that her abilities and meager resources were insufficient to deliver her family from the debtors.

When Elisha asked what she had in her house, her response was "nothing there at all," and then she quickly added, "except a little oil" (2 Kings 4:2 NIV).

Always try to find the silver lining in your situation. The Word shows that there will always be one, and it will be more than sufficient to transform your circumstance (1 Corinthians 10:13; Psalm 37:25).

Elisha then asked her to borrow as many buckets as possible, return to the privacy of her house, and fill the buckets from the little oil she had. Some people would have walked away from him upset. Having been told it was a meager amount of oil, where would the extra supply come from? If the miracle did not occur, how much embarrassment would she and her family face when their neighbors found out? Would they call them names? We often contend with such thoughts whenever a miracle is coming our way. If we do not overcome those thoughts by faith, we will miss the miracle. Miracles represent divine excellence, and they come into our lives only by faith.

The widow believed the man of God and did exactly as he commanded. The oil did not stop flowing until all the borrowed vessels were filled. When she returned to report the miracle to Elisha, he asked her to sell the oil and use some of the proceeds to pay her debt. Her family would live off the balance.

God never gives just enough. He always exceeds expectation. We should embrace the true spirit of excellence both in terms of what we expect of God and what others expect of us.

The little boy who gave five loaves of bread and two fishes to the disciples of Christ also gave occasion for divine excellence to manifest. The disciples had the enormous challenge of trying to feed over five thousand people. They traversed the crowd in search of food (a silver lining) that would serve as seed for a miracle.

The boy had several other choices. Sharing what he had at the moment was the best thing he could have done. After all of the people were fed, there were twelve baskets left over. Had he not chosen the path of excellence by giving his best, he would never have experienced the honor of being used by God to feed thousands of people (Matthew 14:13-21).

Excellence is a gift from God. As you strive for it in every area of your life, pray for the spirit of excellence. The Hebrew trio is a testimony to the extraordinariness of the spirit of excellence. The king in their days described them as being ten times better than his other advisors because the spirit of excellence was in them.

Tenet 4: Understand that your circumstance is not an accident.

If you are walking in God's will, everything that happens around you serves to prepare you for your intended future. Nothing will happen in your life by accident. Therefore, in whatever situation you find yourself, prayerfully seek God's guidance. He is either teaching you something, correcting a character defect, or building up your faith. He is the potter and you are the clay (Isaiah 64:8). If you are not in shape, it behooves Him to break, soften, and remold you. Though the process may be painful, the pain is negligible compared to the blessings that await those who endure. Your attitude should therefore be to let your faith shine in every situation. It both glorifies God and puts the enemy in his place.

Jacob's struggles with his father-in-law illustrate the need to approach every experience with faith and godly wisdom. He had reached an agreement with Laban to serve him for seven years so he could marry Rachel, the younger of his two daughters. When the time expired, Laban reneged on his promise by offering Leah, his first daughter.

Jacob could have walked out on Laban and his daughters. Had he done that, he would have missed out on significant preordained blessings. He also had the option of abducting Rachel. But Laban could easily have found and punished him. Instead, he humbled himself and settled for working another seven years (Genesis 29:15-30). That was his desired future and he was willing to endure whatever was necessary to achieve it. He too had twice cheated his brother out of his rightful blessings. It seemed as though he needed another couple of years to rid himself of trickery. It worked! God got his attention and he went back and made peace with his brother (Genesis 33:1-19).

Moses is another good example of how God uses our circumstances to orchestrate His will for our lives. He had not always been the meekest man who ever lived. He had a major problem with anger that took forty years of wilderness training to correct. At the end of that period, he had been shaped into the leader God wanted him to be.

Make the best of every situation because your purpose is tied to it. This generation is prone to finding the easiest, shortest, and quickest way to escape every unpleasant experience. However, in the quest for a quick fix, you can delay or even sabotage your destiny. The people of Israel could have been in the wilderness for only a few days. But in the effort to assert their will, they continually disobeyed God, and as a consequence, they were stuck there for forty years.

Tenet 5: Get an early start.

People who are always late never experience all of their blessings. Consider this statement in Proverbs 8:17: "Those that seek me early shall find me" (NIV). This is the Lord advising us to look for Him early so we do not spend much of our lives sauntering in darkness and wondering about what could have been. He further implies that if we do not seek Him early, we may never find Him. Nothing would please the devil more than to steal people's lives as they revel in disobedience. It profits nothing to gain the whole world and lose one's soul (Matthew 16:26).

Sometimes, we suffer unnecessarily when we are not early. The prodigal son had forgotten all about his father until poverty struck. Though he should never have deserted his family, he could have realized his poor judgment much sooner than he did. However, as soon as homelessness, loneliness, and hunger struck, he made the right decision. As the Lord declares, "In their affliction they will seek me early" (Hosea 5:15 KJV). Knowing that our future depends on the relationship we have with Him, why would we want to endure pain before we seek Him?

Solomon admonishes us to remember our Creator when we are young (Ecclesiastics 12:1). Most young people have enough strength to match their passion. They also have more years to be able to accomplish God's plan for their lives. The sooner they are ready, the earlier they will be available for the Master's use.

At the end of an annual feast in Jerusalem, Jesus stayed behind because He was discussing the Scriptures with religious leaders. Since He was only twelve, His family was deeply troubled that they had lost Him. When they eventually found Him, He told them that He needed to be about His Father's business (Matthew 2:41-49).

As a teenage boy, David defeated the wild animals that came

after his flock, and in the process, he learned critical lessons for fighting formidable opponents. He learned that faith would overcome any obstacle. Thus, when all of Israel's army retreated from Goliath, he stood and humiliated the giant. His action had a greater significance than rescuing Israel's army; it earned him national acclaim, which was needed to establish legitimacy with the people for his future role as king.

An important way to assure that we experience all that God has planned for us is to get an early start.

Tenet 6: Effectively manage the unexpected.

Relentless preparation is the most effective approach to managing the unknown. It minimizes the tendency to worry about a potential threat or opportunity and increases the chances of having a desirable outcome. This does not mean that we have to become a jack-of-all-trades. Instead, it implies that we must focus on whatever God has given us to do and be as proficient at it as possible.

The Word admonishes us to be prepared at all times to share the gospel (Ephesians 6:15). We do not always have the opportunity to plan an encounter with an unbeliever. We should be prepared to deliver the Word whenever the Spirit of God leads us to do so.

Jesus counseled us to be watchful because He will return unexpectedly (Matthew 24:42). We should be in a constant state of preparedness. Even if we neglect all other areas of our lives, we cannot overlook our relationship with Him, as the consequence can be eternally devastating.

Resilience Development

CHAPTER 10

Staying the Course

In pursuing God's purpose for your life, it's not necessarily the things you start that count, but the things you finish. The world boasts of many starters: aspiring students, hopeful lovebirds, budding entrepreneurs, potential artists. For some, these visions of a promising future exist only in the realm of the imagination. They start the thought process but never take any action to actualize it. Others manage to take a step or two toward translating their thoughts into action, but many never follow through. Students hop from one program or school to another. Some earn a reputation as "professional students" due to their inability to graduate in a reasonable time frame. Folks who can't see enough of each other vow to live together until separated by death. But some 50 percent of them end up breaking that vow in fewer than ten years. Promising entrepreneurs and artists come up with new ideas all the time. But often the only evidence of their dogged efforts is a long trail of abandoned ventures.

It's not that these people don't desire to finish what they start. Usually, people don't set out to fail. However, when vital preparatory steps are ignored or missed, especially if godly principles are left out, lasting success will always be elusive. A person cannot achieve the future God has purposed for him if he doesn't have a relationship with Him. A divine purpose requires divine favor to materialize, and as the Bible points out, sin will prevent divine favor from entering our lives (Jeremiah 5:25).

If you find yourself in the above situation, revisit the first two sections of the book. They outline the process for setting your destiny on the right course and revoking your Achilles' heel.

This chapter is primarily for two categories of people:

a.   Those who already have a relationship with the Lord but are having difficulties with sustaining success;

b.   Those who have become successful and desire to stay that way.

If you identify with the first category, recognize that ignorance is often the biggest obstacle to sustaining success. As the Lord put it, "My people are destroyed for lack of knowledge" (Hosea 4:6). The lacking knowledge refers to the principles for sustaining success. And you cannot identify or deal with your pitfalls until you understand these principles.

If, on the other hand, you've taken the right steps and as a result have begun to experience the unfolding of the divine will for your life, upholding the principles that brought the success is vital. To these principles we now turn.

Principles for sustaining success.

Put God first. If you desire to remain successful, the most critical and enduring requirement is to always put God first. Anything that causes you to compromise your faith, or subtract from the resources you would normally devote to God, is effectively taking His place in your life. When you muffle truth for a quick win, or allow the thrill of success to adversely impact your relationship with God, you're allowing your desires to displace Him.

For example, if you allow a new job, home, or car to consume the time you would have spent doing God's work, you're saying, by your actions, that the gift is more important than the Giver. If you fail to patiently wait on God to fulfill His promise to you, or if you deliberately ignore the Word to gratify self, you're essentially telling God that you don't need Him to bring those blessings into your life. You're also opening the door to pain and regret. That's what happened to Abraham when he impregnated his maidservant because he and Sarah would no longer wait on God for the promised child. In the end, God ordered Abraham to separate his family from the maidservant and his illegitimate son. This separation caused him great anguish. But that is what happens when we override God.

David had a similar experience when he gave priority to a lascivious appetite. That decision led to adultery, murder, and an illegitimate child. However, the child died as a consequence of divine judgment (2 Samuel 11:1-27; 12:1-23).

It is detrimental to seek a shortcut to your blessing if God has already promised it to you. He has never failed and will never fail to fulfill His promises (Hebrews 10:23; 1 Thessalonians 5:24).

Focus on the vision. Focus on the vision God has given you. It's easy for people to lose focus and, in the process, divest themselves of their vision. Take King Saul, for instance. God anointed him king over Israel, and he reigned successfully until envy set in. Instead of concentrating on his purpose, the hunt for David became an all-consuming diversion. It eventually evolved into his primary mission. Although he knew he was out of favor with God, he continued unrepentantly. He was intransigent to the point that when he needed guidance, he bypassed God and sought help from a fortune teller. The fortune teller communicated the judgment that took his life (1 Samuel 10:17-27; 19:1-24; 28:3-25; 31:1-6).

Eli had a solid start as priest. But the responsibilities of his office took on so much significance that his relationship with God suffered. Over time, he was hardly able to decipher God's voice. His loss of focus was reflected in his children's lives in that he failed to teach them the ways of God.

In the meantime, he regularly performed the rituals of priesthood. In fact, he was engaged enough to observe in his congregation what looked like an alcoholic writhing from inebriation.

His children eventually became a menace to the congregants. They forced fornication on the women and desecrated sacrifices that were offered to God. Not surprisingly, their behavior brought a curse on his entire family. But even after the curse was pronounced, he didn't stop to take stock of what went wrong or take penitent and corrective measures that might have appealed to God's mercy. Instead, he continued unfazed in his priestly routine.

Eli teaches us to be careful about our passions. It helps to stop every so often to ask yourself why you do what you do every day. It's how you can ensure that you're still being driven by the right reason.

Not until the Philistines defeated Israel in a battle and stole the ark of God did Eli realize God's glory had departed. The child who was born to Hophni, one of his sons, was named Ichabod, which means that God's glory had departed from His people (1 Samuel 4:20-22).

All around us there are priests, pastors, elders, deacons, and other Christian leaders who, after having had an initial success, lost sight of the reason for their calling. For some, the love of money has all but erased their vision. We are witnesses to a generation where many preachers are much better fundraisers than they are communicators of the Word. They often speak of faith, but not when it comes to trusting God to meet their financial needs. They must keep the pressure on or God's people will not give. They forget that, by faith, the apostles accomplished all they did and had more than they ever needed.

Like Saul and Eli, these so-called men and women of God look and talk the part, but "Ichabod" is written in bold over their lives. As Paul observed, they have a form of godliness, but deny the underlying power (2 Timothy 3:5). Sadly, some of the most unwelcome people in their lives are those who have been led of God to expose their sin or bring them to order. Their experiences are often similar to Micaiah's when, in speaking the truth, he contradicted hundreds of other prophets. All of Ahab's prophets had prophesied favorably about an impending battle. But Micaiah, whom Ahab hated and other prophets despised, prophesied otherwise. When he was done speaking, Zedekiah, one of the prophets, slapped him in the face for speaking out of turn (1 Kings 22:24).

Compromised preachers often use the pulpit as a weapon to humiliate and excoriate those who stand for the truth. Since their motivation is not of God, their tirades become a seed of discord. If they continue in their self-serving ways, they will become like the scribes and Pharisees who would not enter into the kingdom nor allow others to enter (Matthew 23:13).

Men and women laboring in the Lord's vineyard must remember that they represent the almighty God on earth. They must remember that judgment will begin in the house of God. Those who abuse their office for personal gain won't escape punishment. Speaking through Jeremiah, the Lord said this about them: "Because you have scattered my flock and driven them away and have not bestowed care on them, I will bestow punishment on you for the evil you have done" (Jeremiah 23:2 NIV).

Great servants of God get off track sometimes. But the secret to their survival is not to let pride get in the way. Abraham, Isaac, Moses, David, and Peter, to name a few, lost focus at one point or another. The difference between them and the likes of Samson, Saul, and Judas is that they repented and got back on track. If you've gotten off kilter, get on your knees and talk to your heavenly Father about it. He will never overlook a broken and contrite heart (Psalm 51:17).

Don't despise the day of small things. (See Zechariah 4:10.) The fact that you're only experiencing small successes isn't a reason to give up your vision. God's plan for your future isn't a get-rich-quick scheme. Fame and power aren't always built into it. What's required of you is disciplined adherence to the plan and gratitude for whatever success you achieve (1 Thessalonians 5:18). Provided you're walking in obedience, every experience will bring you closer to achieving and living your vision.

After sharing his vision of being in an exalted leadership position, Joseph made a disappointing discovery. His brothers hated him so much, some of them wanted him dead. Before he could digest the unpleasant revelation, he found himself a slave in a foreign country. On the surface, that seemed like the most illogical step toward achieving his lofty vision. But his faith was put to an even greater test when he was unjustly imprisoned in a country where he had no relatives. The only person who could have bailed him out was the one who had put him in jail.

At this point, it would have been reasonable for anyone observing Joseph's life to conclude that he would "never make it" or that he was under a curse. Regardless of the fact that he remained faithful to God, and that he was successful at everything he did, trouble seemed to have had his number on speed dial. It would have been natural for him to have stopped hoping for his intended future. Instead, he did the best he could in every situation. He brought dignity to slavery, excellence to servitude, and character to prison. He walked in excellence and didn't neglect the days of humble beginnings. His faithfulness brought an end to his struggles.

Don't forget your first love. A desirable new venture elicits strong passion and energy. Even if it's fledgling, the owner commits whatever resources he or she can muster to ensure its success. Other initiatives take a backseat until it's up and running. This is similar to the experience of most new Christians. They love the Lord so much, they would do whatever it takes to please Him.

The Bible teaches that you should maintain this level of focus and commitment throughout the execution of your vision. However, it's not uncommon for people to get bogged down in minutia, lose momentum to the pressures and challenges of actualizing a vision, or become lost in the fray of success.

As a solution to these setbacks, Paul instructs us to lay aside every weight so that we can focus on the race ahead of us (Hebrews 12:1). If you desire to retain God's enabling presence, your attention to the plan He gives you must, at all times, be undivided.

If you lose focus God can get your attention in a number of ways. For Moses, it was the miracle of the burning bush. Jonah's was a gruesome familiarity with the inner workings of a live fish.

If the Lord tries to get your attention and you continually ignore or resist Him, you will lose His favor. Ignoring Him continuously may lead to destruction. As Proverbs 29:1 puts it, "A man who remains stiff-necked after many rebukes will suddenly be destroyed—without remedy" (NIV).

In his letter to the church in Ephesus, John reinforced the need to sustain initial momentum. After extolling their labor and patience, he pointed out one major weakness: They had forgotten their "first love." They let the passion and zeal they had when they first accepted Christ dissipate. Consequently, they began to focus on things that didn't count toward their future. John therefore instructed them to repent and return to their first love. If they didn't, he warned that they would lose the presence of God (Revelation 2:4-5).

Develop a succession plan. Staying the course means ensuring that a long-term vision doesn't perish after your demise. It implies creating and successfully implementing a succession plan.

God's plan for you is only a small piece of a much bigger plan. When you've fulfilled your vision, you've accomplished your part. The bigger plan, however, might be a multi-phased, multi-generational plan that takes thousands of years to fully materialize. God's plan for Abraham included provisions for his descendants ad infinitum.

Abraham passed on the vision to Isaac, and Isaac did likewise to Jacob. Through Jacob, the vision was made available to the twelve tribes of Israel. When Israel had leaders who recognized the God of Abraham, Isaac, and Jacob, they were able to continue on the terms of God's covenant with Abraham and therefore enjoyed the accompanying blessings. However, the leaders who ignored those terms brought suffering, bondage, and death to the people. This illustrates the need to commit a vision into capable and trusted hands. To do otherwise may be a disservice to generations yet unborn.

Abraham's vision included blessings for other nations. Jesus became the personification of the blessings to the Gentiles, and everyone who receives Him, regardless of race or nationality, qualifies for them. Therefore, Christ had the enormous responsibility of ensuring that His message got out to the uttermost ends of the earth.

Knowing that He couldn't achieve this by Himself, He selected twelve men to partner with Him in the effort. He subsequently spent as much time as was needed to share His vision with them. In the process, they learned different aspects of His ministry, including aspects that other followers were not privy to. He also gave them opportunities to practice what they were being taught. He was their leader, coach, mentor, friend, and confidant.

When He felt they were ready, He began to unveil details of their post-resurrection responsibilities. Finally, before ascending to heaven, He made provisions for supernatural empowerment so they could achieve their full potential.

In addition to extending Abraham's blessings to us, Christ was demonstrating how to keep a vision alive. First, you need to prayerfully identify individuals who share your vision. You then have to build a trusting relationship with them. You can achieve this by educating them on your plan for actualizing the vision, as well as by having them by your side as the vision translates into tangible results. Let them experience the challenges and rewards with you, and as they mature, discuss future steps with them.

Although Moses and Elijah preceded Christ's earthly ministry, they took this same approach with Joshua and Elisha, respectively. Consequently, both successors were extremely successful.

Remember that your purpose adds value to the lives of others. Seeking ways to perpetuate it will extend its value to a greater number of people.

Remain in a state of readiness. Businesspeople often speak of *kaizen,* or continuous improvement. It entails an ongoing effort to ensure something is as good and useful as it can possibly be at any given point in time. Furthermore, it maximizes efficiency as excesses or deficiencies are constantly being identified and addressed. Processes and products that aren't constantly reviewed for improvement soon become obsolete.

The same principle applies to people. If you don't make an effort to constantly sharpen your skills, you will inevitably fade into obsolescence. The fact that you're the founder or CEO of a company doesn't imply that you've learned all there is to know about your field of endeavor. When circumstances or paradigms change, you need to adapt. Regardless of rank and occupation, only those who have taken the time to prepare themselves will successfully weather the vagaries of unpredicted changes.

In addition to anticipating future knowledge and skill needs, readiness includes planning for physical or material needs of a vision so that when opportunity knocks, you will have the needed resources to take advantage of it.

The parable of the ten virgins is a priceless lesson in the necessity of adequate preparation. In this story, ten virgins were told to await a bridegroom. Each virgin needed a lit lamp to accompany the groom to the wedding. While five of the virgins had oil in their lamps and an additional supply, the other five didn't have extra oil. They didn't anticipate that their oil might run dry. But they were wrong.

The groom was delayed so long that the virgins fell asleep waiting for him. When he finally arrived, all the lamps were out of oil. The virgins who had brought an extra supply were able to immediately refill their lamps. The unprepared ones begged them for some oil, but their plea wasn't honored as the wise virgins wanted to be prepared in case of another eventuality. At the eleventh hour, the foolish virgins went looking for a place to purchase oil. By the time they got back, the wedding door was closed (Matthew 25:1-13).

Receiving an invitation to a wedding, and arriving at the waiting area, were important levels of success for the virgins. However, being prepared for the unexpected made the difference between those who achieved their full potential and those who didn't.

CHAPTER 11

Overcoming Opposition

Opposition must come, and it often comes from places you least expect. The enemy will use anything and anyone to try to stop what God has planned for you. Sometimes, he even uses your family to hinder your success.

For example, the only thing Joseph did to unleash the wrath of his brothers was sharing his dream of a better future. He might have hoped that they would reason with him, perhaps even support him in pursuing it. But they saw the matter differently. The idea of honoring their younger brother pushed them over the edge, and some of them sought to kill him.

As Christ's ministry grew, His fame spread throughout Judah and beyond, and thousands of people began to seek Him out for His uncommon wisdom. They also sought him for salvation, healing, and miracles. Nonetheless, Christ took time to return home to minister to His relatives and fellow Nazarenes. But as He spoke in their synagogue, all they saw was a carpenter's son, a neighborhood kid, and a usurper of the priest's role. As a result, they took offense at Him and rejected His message. Christ made this statement in response to how He was treated: "A prophet is not without honor, except in his own country and in his own house" (Matthew 13:57).

Job also knew what it felt like to contend with opposition from a family member. In the moments when he most needed support from his beloved wife, she ridiculed him and advised that he curse God before he died (Job 2:9). The person he trusted most wrote him off and trivialized his faith—his only source of solace and succor.

Your closest friends, teammates, and confidants might be the ones who rise against you. Judas ate from the same plate and drank from the same cup as Jesus. Yet he hardly blinked when he saw an opportunity to benefit from betraying his master. People on a seemingly close-knit team can have separate and contradictory agendas.

Of the twelve spies whom Moses sent to Canaan, only Joshua and Caleb gave a report that validated God's plan for Israel. The report of the other ten instigated the people to oppose the plan. They stirred up so much resentment that Moses' best efforts to change the people's minds were met with stiff resistance. The resistance eventually cost the majority of the people their intended future.

Saul couldn't have asked for a more faithful and loyal follower than David. The young lad treated him like a father, mentor, senior friend, and confidant. Moreover, David's intervention in a battle saved Saul from a major embarrassment. Yet as soon as it became obvious that God's favor was on David, Saul became viciously jealous and turned against him. He subsequently made several attempts to take David's life.

Opposition to your God-given future can even come from churches, religious leaders, and faith-professing people. Jesus experienced some of His toughest oppositions from the Pharisees, Sadducees, scribes, and priests. They became indignant when He forgave sin, opposed Him when He did good work on a Sabbath, and resisted His teachings as blasphemous. Ultimately, the Pharisees plotted to destroy Him, and while on trial before Pilate, the chief priest incited the crowd to demand His life. (See Matthew 12:14; 27:20.)

Christ's experience highlights the fundamental difference between religion—that is, the carnal observance of ritualistic traditions in honor of deity—and the sincere, individual, spiritual relationship with God through Christ, which is Christianity. Though outside the scope of this work, the fundamental issue with religion is that it focuses so much on the outward manifestation of a spiritual relationship that the reason for the relationship is frequently ignored. But as the Bible clearly states, only those who are alive in the spirit can walk hand-in-glove with God (John 4:24; Galatians 5:16).

Eli was a priest who lost his spiritual connection. During one of the annual prayer gatherings he presided over, he wrongly accused a woman who was pouring out her heart to God. Hannah was determined to bring an end to her barrenness and wouldn't leave God's presence until she received the answer she was looking for. But as she writhed in agony, Eli, the man whose role it was to intercede for her, interrupted her devotion and accused her of being drunk. As God's ambassador in that gathering, his action was most disconcerting. Had Hannah not had a strong relationship with the Father, and had she not been able to discern that it wasn't God speaking, she might have lost faith (and invariably, her blessing) on the spot.

Your opposition may come from political authorities. Several Pharaohs over the years did everything they could to keep God's people from gaining their freedom. One ordered the killing of all males at birth, and when the newborn males that survived prospered, he subjected them to inhuman working conditions. When God instructed that it was time for His people to leave, the sitting Pharaoh responded by multiplying the people's pain and torture (Exodus 1:16; 5:3-13).

Ahab's wife tried to use her position of authority to stop Elijah. She threatened him with death because he was obedient to the will of God.

From childhood, Jesus faced several oppositions from authorities. Herod wanted to kill Him at birth, so he ordered every child less than two years of age in his kingdom to be killed. As Jesus' ministry blossomed, several attempts were made by religious and political leaders to stop Him. At the appointed time, they condemned and crucified Him.

The enemy will stop at nothing to steal or destroy God's purpose for you. *The greater the plan God has for you, the more detrimental it will be to the enemy's agenda, and the more desperately he will try to stop you.*

God's promise to bless the entire world through Abraham would not have been fulfilled if Israel was annihilated. The opportunity for humanity to be reconciled with God would have been destroyed had Jesus been killed at birth. The spreading of the gospel would have suffered significantly had the disciples and the apostle Paul died prematurely. However, in all these cases, the enemy failed, and God's people achieved their purpose.

Why does opposition come?

Why would people who have been called, cleansed, and empowered by the Most High face opposition? There are two primary reasons Christians face opposition.

a. The chief reason we face opposition is the devil's determination to prevent us from experiencing the future God has prepared for His children. He lost his future when he coveted God's throne. Instead, he was sentenced to eternal condemnation. Ever since, his plot has been to steal, kill, and destroy God's children, and to ensure that as many people as he could deceive would share his fate.

b. Opposition can come when we expose an area of our lives to the devil. Exposure in this regard comes from not studying the Word, having a weak prayer life, leading a noncommittal Christian life, or harboring a recurrent sin or outright disobedience. Any of these behaviors will put a hole in the wall of protection that surrounds you and give the enemy an opening to attack and an occasion to rejoice.

When we expose ourselves, the enemy can hurt us. Under Joshua's leadership, the people of Israel suffered a major setback in pursuing their goal of reaching the Promised Land. Ai defeated them, killing a number of their men. They were defeated because Achan's sin exposed them to the enemy.

How do we overcome opposition?

First and foremost, we must understand that opposition is a spiritual matter. The Bible notes that "we wrestle not against flesh and blood, but against principalities, against powers, against the rulers of the darkness of this world, against spiritual wickedness in high places" (Ephesians 6:12 KJV). The person standing in our way, the individual we can see and touch, is *not* the enemy. Wittingly or unwittingly, that person is being used as an instrument in the hands of the devil. If we lose sight of the real enemy and focus on the person, we will end up being frustrated, or falling into sin, which is precisely what Satan hopes for.

There is an ongoing spiritual warfare between the kingdom of God and the kingdom of darkness; between good and evil. All those who have not accepted Christ are captive to the kingdom of darkness. Satan already has them in his back pocket and can do with them as he pleases, his ultimate goal being to keep them from ever making peace with their Creator.

But when we accept Christ as Lord and Savior, we make a spiritual declaration that gets the devil's attention. He sees us as defectors and sends his forces to stop us. If we fail to take our faith seriously, or if we backslide, our latter state will be worse than the former. (See Mathew 12:43-45.) However, when we live in obedience, and take every aspect of our relationship with God seriously, no plot of the enemy against us will succeed. The promise in Isaiah 54:17, "No weapon formed against you shall prosper," will work for us. Jesus stated that we could handle snakes (confront dangerous situations) and they won't hurt us. And even if we are fed poison, it will cause us no harm (Mark 16:18).

Living in obedience requires that we follow God's prescription for victory. Specifically, it requires that we put on His body armor. This armor includes a belt of *truth*, a breastplate of *righteousness*, feet that are always ready to *share the gospel*, and a helmet of *salvation* (Ephesians 6:10-17). "Above all," Paul writes, "taking the shield of *faith* with which you will be able to quench all the fiery darts of the wicked one" (vs. 16, emphasis mine). He further instructs us to take "the sword of the Spirit, which is the *word of God*" (vs.17, emphasis mine). The enemy can and will hurt us if we forget, neglect, or compromise any part of this spiritual armor.

As with any soldier, we need strength to carry our armor. A prayerful Christian is a powerful Christian. Indeed, our strength comes from waiting on the Lord in prayer. (See Isaiah 40:31.) Paul made this point immediately following his instructions on spiritual armor. He enjoined us to always pray in the Spirit. Before Paul, Jesus counseled us to watch and pray that we might not fall into temptation (Matthew 26:41). *There is no substitute for prayer.*

Once we've put on our protective gear, we must turn our attention to the proper action and attitude in confronting opposition. We must understand that the battle is not ours to fight. Attempting to defend ourselves by our own knowledge and strength is tantamount to usurping God's role. We will only complicate the situation and create more problems.

Peter exemplified this point when he cut off one of the ears of a man who was with the crowd that came to arrest Jesus. Although he had the good intention of protecting his master, the arrest was part of Christ's purpose on earth, and he would have gotten in the way by attempting to prevent it. Consequently, Jesus cautioned him for the ill-advised action and noted that God could have sent legions of angels to fight for Him. Afterward, He touched and healed the ear (John 18:10-11; Luke 22:51).

The Bible tells us that our battles are God's; those who fight against us fight against Him (Exodus 14:14; 2 Chronicles 16:9; 20:15; Psalm 60:12). He promises to be an enemy to our enemy (Exodus 23:22). Thus, whenever we are confronted by the enemy, we are to turn the situation over to Him in prayer. We should confess His promises and be attentive to the direction of the Holy Spirit.

This is where most of us fail. Like Peter, we are often so eager to pursue what we think is the right response that we fail to wait on God. Jesus commands us to love our enemies, and to do good to those who hate us (Matthew 5:44). Victory comes only from waiting on God's timing and direction.

Worrying or despairing during a spiritual battle is evidence of fear and faithlessness, and an invitation to satanic oppression. Instead of singing the soliloquy of the oppressed—that is, bemoaning our fate in fear of the unknown—we ought to rejoice and celebrate our victory. Scripture declares that we are already "more than conquerors" (Romans 8:37). The Lord knows every hair on our heads, and not one of them will fall off without His knowing (Matthew 10:30; Luke 21:18).

Furthermore, Jesus promises that if we present our needs to the Father in His name, we will receive whatever we ask for. The Father has prepared a table before us in the presence of our enemy, and come what may, we shall sit at it and eat from it (Psalm 23:5).

Remember that you are never alone. God is always with us, and in His infinite wisdom, He will do whatever is needed to deliver us from the snare of the enemy. As His children marched out of Egypt, the Bible records that He shielded them with a pillar of cloud during the day and a pillar of fire at night (Exodus 13:21).

When Elisha was surrounded by the Syrian army, his servant became worried. He failed to see how he and his master could possibly overcome the large number of highly trained soldiers who surrounded them. But Elisha, knowing the exceeding power of the God he served, told his servant that the army that was for them was far greater than the one against them. When he still didn't believe, Elisha prayed that God might open his eyes. "Then the Lord opened the eyes of the young man, and he saw. And behold, the mountain was full of horses and chariots of fire all around Elisha" (2 Kings 6:17).

The Lord's army always stands ready to do battle on our behalf. When the enemy comes surging like a flood, the Spirit of the Lord will raise a standard against him (Isaiah 59:19). No matter how he comes or where he shows, we will prevail!

Therefore, the right attitude toward opposition is to take a faith position and confidently proceed with what the Lord has called you to do.

What does God do with your opposition?

Although it seems obvious that trying to fight against God is imprudent, people challenge Him all the time. When they stand in the way of His children, they are touching the "apple of His eye" (Zechariah 2:8). Imagine if an opponent came close enough to touch your eye. Your reflexes would probably kick in before his finger reached your face. How much more do you think God will do to defend His precious children!

Speaking of Himself, Jesus said that "whosoever shall fall on this stone shall be broken: but on whomsoever it shall fall, it will grind him to powder" (Matthew 21:44 KJV). To fall on Christ is to die to sin and pick up the new life He offers. Christ falling on someone represents judgment on those who stand in His way.

Below are a few approaches that God employs in dealing with opposition. They are meant to give you an idea of what God can do to ensure your safety, well-being, and progress.

Warning. The king of Syria was upset at how God was using Elisha to reveal his secrets to his enemy, the king of Israel. So he sent people to spy on the prophet, hoping to find a way to obstruct his ministry. After discovering where he lived, the king of Syria sent hundreds of soldiers to arrest Israel's king. He knew Elisha was a powerful prophet. What he didn't know was that because Elisha was fulfilling his God-given purpose, all the armies in the world couldn't have stopped him.

When Elisha saw the soldiers, he prayed blindness upon them. Contrary to their plan of picking him up, he gained the upper hand and led them into the hands of their enemy. He subsequently advised the king of Israel to send them back to their king as a warning. The Syrians never troubled Israel afterward (2 Kings 6:8-23).

Consequences. When Pharaoh's army went after the people of Israel as they were leaving Egypt, God put an impenetrable wall between them and His people. He set them up so they would follow His people onto the miraculous road through the Red Sea. But the road wasn't made for them; it was for the people they sought to destroy.

As they came closer, God took the wheels off their chariots to slow their movement. Then the ground began to cave in. At this point, they realized God was fighting for His people, and they wanted to turn around. But it was too late. They had failed to learn from all the warnings they were given in Egypt. In the end, heavy winds and high waves swallowed them (Exodus 14:1-31).

Confusion. King Jehoshaphat experienced God's deliverance in a remarkable way. When the descendants of Moab and Ammon conspired to attack him, he took the right step by going before the Lord in prayer. The Lord assured Jehoshaphat that he wouldn't need to fight in the battle. He, Jehovah, would deliver him from the hand of the enemy.

Heartened by the news, Jehoshaphat took a rather unusual step. Instead of having the army lead the march to war, he put the choir in the front! He was so confident in God that all he could do was to give Him praise. As the choir approached the battleground, God threw confusion into the camp of the enemy, and they turned on one another. They didn't stop until the last one of them was dead. Thus, the only work that Jehoshaphat and his army had to do was to gather up the spoils.

Return to sender. Under King Ahasuerus, Mordecai, a God-fearing Jew, faced an opposition that only God could have defeated. Haman, the king's chief of staff, plotted to have Mordecai hanged, even though his only offense was that he didn't bow down and reverence Haman.

Although he was richer and more powerful than Mordecai, Haman became angry every time he saw this Jew. The enemy had planted a seed of hatred in his heart toward Mordecai, and as a result, he wanted to hurt him at all cost. He built a seventy-five-feet-high gallows from which he intended to hang Mordecai. However, as he was plotting, God was watching. When the gallows was completed, circumstances turned around, and instead of Mordecai, Haman was hanged on it (Esther 5:12-14; 7:10)!

Final thought.

God's declaration that the wicked won't go unpunished is as potent as it is sobering. He is patient and merciful and allows them a great deal of opportunity to repent. However, if they don't turn from their wicked ways, He won't sit back and watch them destroy His children's future. He will fight for us!

CHAPTER 12

The Wisdom of Sharing

S haring is one of the most significant principles of sustaining success.

The process of exchange enables all of creation to function in harmony. It's the avenue by which each element interacts with the others, releasing one form of benefit for another. If one element malfunctions, its impact permeates the others.

If, for instance, the sun lost its luminosity, life as we know it would be fatally disrupted. The earth needs sunlight to support its various life forms; plants need it to produce food and oxygen, and humans and animals need food and oxygen to survive. In turn, humans and animals exhale carbon dioxide, which is critical to plant growth and survival.

Reproduction also occurs through a process of exchanging potent forces between male and female within a species. Even in hermaphrodites, this sharing has to occur, albeit within one entity, for an offspring to emerge.

Indeed, all of creation is an amazing web of interdependent relationships. None of it was designed as a stand-alone entity.

Eternal life comes from sharing.

The most fundamental and critical goal in life, salvation, cannot be achieved until someone shares the gospel. Jesus left His throne, took on mortality, lived among us, and gave His life for only one reason: to remove the curse of sin and give us eternal life.

Before His ascension, He commissioned every believer to engage in propagating the gospel (Matthew 28:18-20). People will not repent of their sins unless they are told of the inherent danger in failing to do so, and the glorious future that awaits those who do.

In his letter to the Romans, Paul states that "everyone who calls on the name of the Lord will be saved" (Romans 10:13 NIV). But in verse 14 he raises some critical questions: "How, then, can they call on the one they have not believed in? And how can they believe in the one of whom they have not heard? And how can they hear without someone preaching to them?"

Sadly, many Christians lack the will, understanding, and savvy to effectively share the gospel. Some erroneously believe responsibility for spreading the Word rests solely with the clergy. Others hesitate for reasons that include fear, personal idiosyncrasies, and cultural barriers. Whatever the excuses may be, thousands of people are denied the gospel as a result.

Sometimes God will bring people your way so you can minister the Word to them. When you disobey, you're denying them a shot at salvation, which is the most needful thing for them.

An angel appeared to Philip and instructed him to go to the road between Jerusalem and Gaza. When he arrived there, he saw an official of the Ethiopian government riding in his chariot. The Spirit of God instructed Philip to join the official in the chariot. When he approached, he heard him reading a line from Isaiah and asked if he understood the prophet's message. The official responded that he wouldn't understand unless someone explained it to him. Seizing the opportunity, Philip explained the passage and preached the gospel to him. When he was done, the official accepted Jesus and was baptized the same day (Acts 8:26-40).

Had Philip ignored the Spirit of God or hesitated about approaching the high-ranking official in his private wagon, the official might have been lost forever. Jesus made a salient point in this regard: If we're ashamed to discuss Him in this world, He will be ashamed to include us when He returns for His saints (Luke 9:26).

Aside from directly sharing the Word, there are several other ways Christians can share their faith. Jesus called His followers the salt of the earth (Matthew 5:13). If you're salt, it makes sense that you would want to add flavor to people's lives. Christianity is a calling to an exemplary life; your conduct and interaction are modeled after Christ's. Christ wants us to be at a place where His beauty radiates so much through us it causes others to desire what we have.

Christians are also called the light of the world (Matthew 5:14). Light that is hidden serves no purpose. The world should look to us for direction, hope, and leadership.

Share your asset.

Jesus pronounced an ageless principle in the statement that "it is more blessed to give than to receive" (Acts 20:35 NRSV). There are great blessings in sharing our assets or resources, including talent, time, property, and money. God expects us to give according to His blessings in our lives (Deuteronomy 16:17).

From a carnal perspective, we have less when we give. But in reality, God gives us exponential returns for our giving. The Bible affirms this promise in Luke 6:38: "Give, and it will be given to you: good measure, pressed down, shaken together, and running over." Giving is an act of faith, and when we fail to give, we won't experience the superabundance that results from a generous spirit.

The widow of Zarephath demonstrates how the principle of giving can yield tremendous results. In a period of severe drought, when people were starving to death, this woman was preparing a last meal for herself and her son when Elijah stopped by. He asked for a cup of water and some food. She responded that the only food available was their last meal. The man of God asked her to prepare his meal first, and afterward, to prepare theirs.

She didn't argue with the prophet. She was willing to obey and trust her situation to God. After she served Elijah, her flour and oil were continuously replenished until the end of the drought. By being faithful in giving, she and her son miraculously survived the drought. (See 1 Kings 17.)

One of the most difficult assets for us to share is time. We're so

preoccupied with our daily routines that the Lord's business sometimes takes a backseat. Some of us try to substitute money for time.
However, there are circumstances when no amount of money can
replace our presence. The difference between the Good Samaritan
and the other passersby was that he took the time to care for the
robbed and wounded man. Had he walked by like the others, the
man might have bled to death on the roadside (Luke 10:30-37).

Required sharing.

Being the source of all good and perfect gifts, God requires that
we honor Him with tithes (a tenth of our earnings) and offerings.
Giving tithes and offerings is an act of obedience. It is also a means
of affirming our trust in God, tapping into His blessings, and
supporting His work.

Abraham gave a tenth of all his profits to God (Genesis 14:20).
He also gave generously at other times, even to the point of willingly offering his son out of obedience. As a result, everything he
did prospered tremendously.

Unfaithfulness in the area of giving is tantamount to robbing
God (Malachi 3:8) and, therefore, an open invitation to a curse (vs.
9). As a consequence of this curse, the devourer moves in and
attacks the jobs, finances, investments, health, and other areas of the
robbers' lives. It is not unusual for them to constantly struggle to
make ends meet. Haggai 1:6 describes their condition in clear
terms: "You have planted much, but have harvested little. You eat,
but never have enough. You drink, but never have your fill. You put
on clothes, but are not warm. You earn wages, only to put them in a
purse with holes in it" (NIV).

Often, unfaithfulness to God in the area of giving is indicative
of other problems. For Cain, the underlying problem that precipi-
tated his stingy offering was greed. The same was true for Ananias
and Sapphira. They lied about their giving to cover their true intention of not wanting to part with some of their proceeds.

If you struggle in the area of giving, I encourage you to examine
your life to determine if there is an underlying problem. Until the
root cause is addressed, you may never enjoy freedom in this area
of your Christian walk.

The only way to break free from the curse that results from not giving as the Lord has commanded is to begin to obey His command. When you do, He promises to open the floodgates of heaven and pour out so much blessing you won't have enough room for it (Malachi 3:10). What's more, He will prevent the devourer from stealing your blessings (vs. 11).

Proper attitude toward giving.

With God, it's not how much we give (after tithing) that counts. Jesus once observed a gathering of givers as they cast their offerings and noticed a poor widow drop a penny in the offering basket. He later told his disciples that the widow gave more than everyone else in the group because she trusted God with all she had. Giving is a way of showing that we trust God. The greater our trust in Him, the more blessings He will entrust to us.

God isn't a fan of miserly givers. Cain was a farmer and Abel a shepherd. When they went to make an offering to the Lord, Abel sacrificed the choicest of the firstborns of his herd, and the Lord respected his offering. But Cain cared little about what he gave to God, and consequently, his offering was rejected. "God loves a cheerful giver" (2 Corinthians 9:7). If we want our giving to be acceptable to Him, our hearts must be in it.

Publicizing our giving will rob us of our blessings. Jesus said that by seeking praise and recognition, people who make a public display of their giving won't be rewarded by the Father (Matthew 6:1). Giving, especially almsgiving, should be done as discreetly as possible.

Christ said that, when we give, the right hand must not know what the left hand is doing (vs. 3). Our intent should be to glorify God, not self.

Being dishonest with our giving can be detrimental to our lives. Ananias and his wife, Sapphira, were members of the early church. At that time the church was of one heart and the people lived communally; that is, members willingly shared their possessions with one another.

Wanting to fit in, this couple sold some of their property to give to the church. But they lied about the proceeds and lost their lives as a result (Acts 5:1-11). It is better not to give at all than to give out of compulsion or to lie about giving.

Share your testimony.

A testimony is proof of an experience or event.

It is also an account of divine enablement or intervention. The Bible is a testimony to the redeeming power of God, and a saved person can testify to the life-changing potential of God's power. When thieves, prostitutes, crooked businesspeople, pervert leaders, or just plain old sinners on a downward spiral to hell turn over a new leaf upon receiving Christ into their lives, their testimonies can spark hope in others and cause them to seek the Savior.

On the day of Pentecost, the Holy Spirit descended on the disciples of Christ and caused them to speak in diverse tongues. People who heard the different languages invited others, and in no time a crowd grew around them. The people weren't sure what to make of the event. While some were amazed, others mocked the disciples, thinking they were drunk.

Raising his voice, Peter addressed the crowd. He reminded them of the Savior they had crucified and the message of reconciliation He brought. Among other references to the Old Testament, he cited Joel 2:28, affirming that what they were witnessing was evidence of that verse of Scripture. When he was finished speaking, about three thousand people gave their lives to Christ (Acts 2:14-41)! The impact of his message teaches us never to underestimate the power of a testimony.

Our testimonies are critical to living a victorious Christian life. John points out in Revelation 12:11 that we overcome our accuser by the blood of Jesus and the word of our testimony.

The devil cannot withstand or annul a true testimony, as God will always defend His name. King Saul initially rejected David's request to confront Goliath. But after David shared his testimony—how, by divine enablement, he had ripped up with his bare hands the bears and lions that sought to prey on his father's flock—Saul's confidence in the young man's ability received a boost and he agreed to have him confront the giant. No sooner had he acquiesced than David stretched his sling and drove a stone into Goliath's temple.

Share love.

True leaders are driven by love. Whether it's love for the Lord, love for people, love for a cause, or all of the above, we can attain our full potential only when love is the basis of our passion. Job was able to endure unspeakable adversity because he loved God. And only love could have persuaded Christ to leave the comfort of divine royalty to serve stray mortals.

Love enables us to muster all the faith, strength, patience, and hope we may need to weather any storm. Note that love in this context is dissimilar from the infatuation that causes a teenage boy to brave the dead of night to steal a second glance at a damsel he met the night before, only to abandon her for the next sultry thing. Nor is this the love that vanishes with the honeymoon phase of marriage. The kind of love I speak of here is *agape* love, God's kind of love. This love emanates from the love of God in us. And it never fails.

Agape love was what Ruth had for her mother-in-law, Naomi. Naomi was very old when her husband and two sons died. Disheartened by the deaths, she decided to return to her home in Judah. But before she left, she blessed her daughters-in-law and released them to return to their homes. When they insisted on staying with her, she reminded them of her sorrowful state and the fact that she couldn't offer them any more sons. Orpah then kissed her good-bye.

But Ruth decided the death of her husband wasn't going to be the end of her relationship with his family. She had been through thick and thin with Naomi, and husband or not, she wasn't going to abandon the poor woman when she needed help the most. She articulated her decision in this selfless and moving statement: "Don't urge me to leave you or to turn back from you. Where you go I will go, and where you stay I will stay. Your people will be my people and your God my God" (Ruth 1:16 NIV). This level of commitment can only spring from true love.

In his letter to the Corinthians, Paul extolled love as the greatest virtue. He provides, in my humble opinion, the most accurate description of *agape* love.

Consider this passage from the Amplified Bible:

If I [can] speak in the tongues of men and [even] of angels, but have not love (that reasoning, intentional, spiritual devotion such as is inspired by God's love for and in us), I am only a noisy gong or a clanging cymbal.

And if I have prophetic powers (the gift of interpreting the divine will and purpose), and understand all the secret truths and mysteries and possess all knowledge, and if I have [sufficient] faith so that I can remove mountains, but have not love (God's love in me) I am nothing (a useless nobody).

Even if I dole out all that I have [to the poor in providing] food, and if I surrender my body to be burned or in order that I may glory, but have not love (God's love in me), I gain nothing.

Love endures long and is patient and kind; love never is envious nor boils over with jealousy, is not boastful or vainglorious, does not display itself haughtily.

It is not conceited (arrogant and inflated with pride); it is not rude (unmannerly) and does not act unbecomingly. Love (God's love in us) does not insist on its own rights or its own way, for it is not self-seeking; it is not touchy or fretful or resentful; it takes no account of the evil done to it [it pays no attention to a suffered wrong].

It does not rejoice at injustice and unrighteousness, but rejoices when right and truth prevail.

Love bears up under anything and everything that comes, is ever ready to believe the best of every person, its hopes are fadeless under all circumstances, and it endures everything [without weakening].

Love never fails [never fades out or becomes obsolete or comes to an end]. As for prophecy (the gift of interpreting the divine will and purpose), it will be fulfilled and pass away; as for tongues, they will be destroyed and cease; as for knowledge, it

will pass away [it will lose its value and be super-
seded by truth].

And so faith, hope, love abide [faith—conviction
and belief respecting man's relation to God and
divine things; hope—joyful and confident expectation of eternal salvation; love—true affection for
God and man, growing out of God's love for and
in us], these three; but the greatest of these is love.
(1 Corinthians 13:1-8, 13.)

True love doesn't keep mute when a friend is going astray. It's
not afraid to confront brutal facts. Jesus said that He rebukes and
disciplines those He loves (Revelation 3:19). His goal is to help
them get back on course. True leaders must love those around them
enough to be sincere with them at all times.

Love constrains us from going overboard and compels us to do
what's right (2 Corinthians 5:14). It is often the only thing that
stands between us and revenge. Consider David's experience. King
Saul and his army traversed several towns and hatched numerous
clandestine plots in their quest to destroy him. But God was on his
side; therefore, Saul never caught up with him. David had two
opportunities to take the king's life. On one of the occasions, he
cornered Saul in a cave. But instead of killing him, he cut off a
piece of his robe as a sign and a warning. Love restrained him.

In the end, God dealt with Saul so that he was no longer a
barrier on the path of David's destiny (1 Samuel 24:1-22; 26:1-25;
31:1-13).

Mentoring as sharing.

A mentor is a coach or advisor who takes an interest in the development of another person. This relationship can enable budding
leaders to foresee and avoid pitfalls, thereby facilitating their journey
toward fulfillment and maximizing positive experiences.

Paul mentored Timothy, teaching him the ways of God. His
efforts to hone Timothy's leadership skills are evident in the two
epistles Paul wrote to him.

On his second missionary journey, Paul brought Timothy along to expose him to international evangelism and help him build credibility with other Christian leaders (Acts 15:36-41). When Paul was satisfied that he had acquired all the necessary skills, he sent him to continue the ministry in Thessalonica (1Thessolonians 3:1-2).

Timothy earned the respect of other Christians and became a successful leader due to the impact Paul had in his life.

Leaders at all levels have had experiences that can be of benefit to others. They would do well to seek out people to whom they can transfer that learning.

We reap what we sow.

An irrefutable spiritual truth is that we reap what we sow (Galatians 6:7). To sow means to invest. Depending on what and where we're investing, we may make a profit, remain stagnant, or lose our investment. When we sow into good ground, we expect first-rate produce. When we sow generously, we anticipate a plentiful harvest. The reverse is true when the ground is scorched or when we sow sparingly.

Rahab, a prostitute, sowed a good seed. The twelve spies Joshua sent to Jericho entered the city from Rahab's house. When the king of Jericho heard of their presence, he ordered their arrest. However, Rahab hid the spies and saved them from the king. She sowed kindness by protecting men who were on a mission for God. As a result, she and her entire family were the only people saved when Jericho was conquered. In addition, she was adopted into the family of God; she is believed to be the Rahab named in the genealogy of Christ (Matthew 1:5).

The Bible teaches us to sow good seeds and to sow at all times as we don't know which seed will catch the best ground (Ecclesiastics 11:6). Remember that every seed you sow, regardless of where you're sowing or whose life you're sowing into, has an implication for you. It paves the way for divine favor to come on you as you progress toward your desired future.

Self-leadership

CHAPTER 13

Understanding Leadership

L eadership is a universal language. People from every nation practice it. Where there is no leadership, people fail—marriages collapse, businesses die, nations suffer. Zechariah 13:7 makes this point quite graphically: "Smite the shepherd, and the sheep shall be scattered" (KJV). Humankind cannot achieve progress without leadership.

Although leadership manifests at all levels of society, the focus in this section is on how it applies at the level of the individual, or what's paraphrased as "self-leadership." Understanding what it means to lead self will enable you to reap the full benefit of the principles espoused in this book.

But first, we must build the right foundation by shedding light on the theoretical origin of leadership. This foundation should provide you with a good handle on the relevance of the concept to your quest for fulfillment.

Courage, wisdom, and knowledge are attributes of good leaders.
Scholars of all ages have attempted to illuminate the concept of leadership. From the celebrated works of such Greek philosophical greats as Socrates (469-399 BC), Plato (429-347 BC), and Aristotle (384-322 BC) to the literary masterpieces of modern and

post-modern thinkers, attempts to study and understand it have been more than a passing challenge. The Greek trio deserves special mention for their pioneer work on knowledge and ethics. They devoted their lives to seeking and unraveling the mysteries of life. Regrettably, none of them lived to see the advent of Christ, who is the consummation of the truth and knowledge they so desperately sought. (See Isaiah 11:2; John 14:6.)

In his most acclaimed work, *The Republic*, Plato addressed leadership in a political setting. He vehemently argued that bravery, wisdom, and knowledge are the hallmarks of the accomplished leader. Only the philosopher king—that is, a person of sound moral integrity with a superior appetite for learning—should possess what political power there is by virtue of his knowledge, wisdom, and strong moral standing.

While Plato's Great Man theory has grown increasingly unpopular, his thought around the need for the leader to be courageous, knowledgeable, and wise foretold three biblical qualities that every leader, religious or secular, must cultivate to be successful.

Joshua's story provides an illustration of how these qualities come together in a leader. As Moses' period in office came to an end, God chose Joshua to lead the Israelites into the Promised Land. Having wandered for several years in the wilderness, Joshua knew reaching Canaan wasn't going to be a walk in the park. There were formidable nations along the way: nations that significantly outnumbered them, that wouldn't surrender or let them through without a fight. Israel would only reach Canaan by divine guidance.

Dealing with the enemies along the way was one thing; dealing with self, or submitting completely to God's will, was another. Joshua needed to make a quality decision, one that every one of us has to make: Should I obey the will of God or assert my own? He understood that God will never cut corners or compromise His position. He will never surrender under pressure or be distracted by obstacles. He was going to follow through on His plan to lead Israel through Jericho, Ai, and all the other nations in the way. His command and expectation was that Joshua do the same.

While it's smart to know the odds against you in every decision, it's better to have a full appreciation for the odds in your favor. Only by weighing both can a person make the right decision. Joshua took comfort in his knowledge of God's awesome power. He knew how God had wrested Israel from Pharaoh's cruel rule. He was familiar with how He made a dry path for them through the Red Sea and the River Jordan. He had seen manna fall from heaven. Thus, with just a little encouragement, he would make the right decision.

That encouragement came in the form of an assurance of divine enablement. Being omniscient, God foreknew Joshua's concerns and addressed them beforehand. "No man shall be able to stand before you all the days of your life; as I was with Moses, so I will be with you. I will not leave you nor forsake you. Be strong and of good courage. . . . Only be strong and very courageous, that you may observe to do according to all the law which Moses My servant commanded you" (Joshua 1:5-7). This was enough to elevate Joshua's courage.

God requires complete and careful adherence to His commands and laws. In verse 7, God instructed Joshua not to "turn from it to the right hand or to the left." In verse 8, He instructed him to meditate on the laws "day and night."

Being knowledgeable in the laws would give him an in-depth understanding of how to achieve the divine purpose for Israel. Beyond the simple challenges of day-to-day activities, it would enable him to establish patterns and relationships, and discover unapparent meaning, in dealing with complex matters. Additionally, knowing the laws would enable him to walk in obedience and enjoy the resulting favor and prosperity.

As many of us do today, Joshua could have picked the laws that were easy to follow or that best suited his preferences. Or he could have defied God and pursued his own agenda. Psalm 107:43 indicates that it takes wisdom to observe God's commands. Only those who apply wisdom—that is, those who have, observe, and rightfully apply knowledge of God's Word—will exceedingly shine in their leadership roles (Daniel 12:3). Having learned wisdom, Joshua was able to walk the straight and narrow path. His success is a testament to the inevitable outcome.

Lead with purpose.

A widely read sixteenth-century Italian philosopher, Machiavelli saw leadership as a means to an end. In his most popular work, *The Prince*, he posited that the leader could use any means at his disposal, moral or amoral, to achieve his goals.

In one provoking illustration, the prince wanted to rein in one of his morally decadent cities. Fearing the citizens would turn against him, he appointed a deputy and authorized him to take whatever measures were necessary to purge the city of immorality. The deputy had great success, but his method incensed the masses.

The prince, wanting to placate the people and retain their support, turned against his right-hand man. He even asked the people what punishment would be befitting for his deputy. Not surprisingly, they asked for his head, and he delivered it to them on a platter!

Some would describe the prince as politically savvy, street smart, or a shrewd leader. Although he didn't use these exact words, Machiavelli's perspective on leadership gave rise to the clichéd but troubling statement, "The end justifies the means." Corrupt, malignant leaders frequently invoke this statement to justify their actions. But ethics has an irreducible place at every level of leadership. Wicked and degenerate leaders inevitably experience the consequences of their actions.

Leadership is not, in itself, an end. Pastors aim to prepare a spotless church for the coming of the Savior. Corporate leaders seek to generate a profit for stockholders. The army general works hard to win every battle. Holders of public office perform the will of their electors or appointers.

Whether or not you have an official title, in some capacity, you're a leader in your home, church, school, and at work. The question you should consider is: What is my purpose as a leader? If you're modeling Christ in whatever organization or position you find yourself in, you're fulfilling the most critical responsibility of leadership.

Although the methods employed to achieve the ends of leadership, from a Christian perspective, are fundamentally different from some of the approaches that spring from the Machiavellian framework, Machiavelli lends credence to the fact that effective leadership is needed to achieve any worthwhile purpose.

Trait counts.

The word *leader* is traceable to the root *leden,* which means "to travel" or "show the way" (Rost, 1991, p. 38). Christ is the way, and He has traveled ahead of us so we can always look to Him for direction. As our leader, He's not asking us to do anything He's not done or endure anything He didn't endure. (See Hebrews 2:18.) By His example, putting yourself through an experience—taking a course, learning a new skill, leading a team, etc.—before you ask others to do the same is a mark of a good leader. You earn the trust, respect, and credibility of your followers by undergoing the experience first.

Although leaders have been around from time immemorial, efforts to formulate a leadership theory didn't gain momentum until the 1900s. Following Plato's tradition, researchers focused on the traits that made leaders successful. Both leaders and followers were analyzed to identify these traits.

Although Plato's traits theory is considered inconclusive in explaining leadership effectiveness, it remains relevant to the making of leaders. Indeed, leadership literature of the 1970s and 1980s has revisited the theory, especially as it relates to the roles of managers versus leaders in achieving organizational success.

Ignoring traits such as temperament, chastity, integrity, justice, and fairness can result in irreparable setback. In addition to not achieving their full potential, those who disregard them have no place in the kingdom of God (Galatians 5:21).

Your trait, or the quality that distinguishes you, should be the Spirit of God in you. The fruit He will bear in your life is "love, joy, peace, longsuffering, kindness, goodness, faithfulness, gentleness, self-control" (vs. 22-23). When this fruit becomes evident in you, your leadership efforts will yield great results.

Behavior counts.

The Bible admonishes us to behave ourselves in a wise, valiant, holy, just, and blameless manner (1 Samuel 18:14; 1 Chronicles 19:13; 1 Thessalonians 2:10). Cultivating these behaviors is the only way we can maintain our divine connection and live beyond reproach.

Secular leadership study didn't seem to catch on to the importance of behavior to leadership success until the 1950s. Scholars began to emphasize the impact of the action and behavior of leaders as a way to understand leadership. These behaviors were categorized into leadership styles.

Two styles emerged as the most prominent due to their impact on leadership effectiveness. They include task orientation and people-and-relationship orientation. House and Mitchell (1974) further analyzed these categories and came up with a typology of four prominent behaviors: *directive* (the tendency to make decisions for others and expect compliance), *participative* (a style that favors sharing decision-making with others), *task oriented* (the tendency to focus on achieving tangible objectives), and *supportive* (emphasis on building and supporting the person as opposed to focusing on a task).

Some early researchers argued that participative and supportive styles produced the best results. They are right. Not only were followers pleased to participate in the decisions that impacted them, but the interest that leaders took in their success and well-being resulted in a high level of satisfaction.

It's a worthwhile effort to examine your own leadership style in light of House's classification. Your goal should be to develop a style that promotes creativity and collaboration. Rigid and autocratic styles stifle initiative and limit the ability of your followers to release their potential.

Situation counts.

Questions soon emerged about the comprehensiveness of the behavioral approach in studying and understanding leadership. Evidence pointed to the conclusion that the same styles didn't yield the same degree of success in every situation. At the same time, researchers found that the environment within which leaders operated and the people they worked with had a significant impact on success. This is a biblical truth. Jesus was able to reveal secrets about His ministry and the kingdom of God when He was alone with His disciples. He could not do that with the crowd (Mark 4:34). When He found Himself in a hostile environment in Nazareth, He could not perform as many miracles as He did in several other towns (Matthew 13:57-58).

In analyzing the impact of modifying styles to match different environments, proponents of the situational theory found that leaders could successfully navigate different situations by adjusting their styles.

Our Lord Jesus is a compassionate leader. Seeing a sea of souls who needed to come to the knowledge of the truth, He had compassion on them (Matthew 9:36). He is also very sympathetic. When He saw people weeping as a result of Lazarus' death, He did something that inspired the shortest verse in the Bible: "Jesus wept" (John 11:35).

However, faced with a situation where the house of God was being turned into a den of thieves, He took aggressive and immediate action to preserve the integrity and sanctity of the temple of God (Matthew 21:12-13).

Christ was able to adjust His style to suit every situation He encountered. As a result, all His outcomes were in fulfillment of His purpose. If we follow His lead, we will build a similar testimony.

Hershey and Blanchard (1977) came up with the most predominant categorization of styles and situations. They built their theory on the model that House developed. They include:

a. *Telling.* This is a high-task (directive, task-oriented) and low-relationship (participative, supportive) behavior. It requires spending a significant amount of time in providing direction, clarifying roles, and defining objectives. It reflects a low trust environment in that followers or subordinates are unable and sometimes unwilling to deliver optimal results on their own. Leading a group of prisoners to acquire and apply new skills, or leading new employees, is a good example.

b. *Selling.* This requires both high-task and high-relationship behavior. Followers are often willing to work with their leaders. However, they usually lack the skill to get the job done. A leader in this category frequently assumes the role of a coach to his or her followers. A leader might adopt this approach in launching a new operation.

c. *Participating.* This requires high-relationship and low-task behavior. Decisions are made jointly by leaders and followers. The trust level is high and the leader essentially acts as a facilitator. This style would work for experienced and committed subordinates.

d. *Delegating.* This is a low-relationship and low-task behavior. The approach requires highly competent and mature followers. The leader is engaged only to the extent that he or she communicates the assignment to be completed. The higher level of maturity and competence required here differentiates it from the preceding approaches.

In your relationships with your superiors and subordinates, practice how to identify these different situations. Then put forth the effort that's needed to generate optimal results. If, for instance, you're a new hire and need lots of direction, raise your hand if it's not forthcoming. Wallowing in silence will lead to frustration and prolong the time it takes for you to be up to speed in your new job.

On the other hand, assuming you've mastered your job, but you have a supervisor who is a micromanager, discuss the participative approach with him or her.

While the situational model illuminated yet another dimension of leadership, it didn't account for cultural variables that may significantly impact a leader's success. For instance, leadership styles may vary in monarchical versus acephalous societies, individualistic versus communal cultures, and religious versus secular systems.

In addition, the model didn't account for gender-based variation in leadership styles. Although there is a lot of debate around these assertions, women are often said to be more relationship focused. They are described as naturally caring, nurturing, and sensitive. Men, on the other hand, are said to be more directive and task oriented.

Shared leadership.

Some researchers took issue with the traditional focus of leadership on the individual leader. They criticized the idea of identifying one hero leader when, from their perspective, both the leader and follower as part of a team could have made equal contributions to success.

In exploring the role of teams in leadership, they found that "leader roles overlapped, complemented each other, and shifted from time to time and person to person" (Barnes and Kriger, 1986, p. 16). The key to success wasn't in the traits or abilities of any single individual. No one person's energy could surpass the synergy that derived from a high-functioning team. According to them, teamwork, not personal traits, essentially accounted for organizational success.

Pluralists took the team concept further by espousing self-managed and self-directed teams. In a nutshell, a self-managed team is one in which members determine their own approach and share leadership responsibility in implementing goals that are defined *outside* the team. In addition to formulating a preferred work approach and having collective responsibility for leading the team, a self-directed team defines its own goals.

The role of teamwork in achieving significant objectives must be underscored. The assertion that a team can achieve more than a single individual is supported by the Scriptures. In fact, Leviticus 26:8 and Deuteronomy 32:30 suggest that a cohesive, high-functioning, and Spirit-filled team will not only achieve more, but is more likely to achieve astronomical results than an individual. Therefore, if you're a team leader, you will be doing the members of your team, your organization, and yourself a huge favor by building a cohesive, high-performing team.

Although the team concept has gained momentum in most organizations, true self-managed and self-directed teams are still few and far between. The vast majority of organizations are structured in a way that accountability mainly rests with the individual. One reason for this might be that it's not as easy to discipline, not to mention fire, an entire team for the same reason that an individual could lose his or her job. A second reason is the fact that while there are creative ways to reward a team, promotions are still vastly determined on an individual basis.

Transformational leadership.

Burns espoused the concept of transformational leadership in 1978. He distinguished transactional leadership—that is, the approach that exchanges reward and recognition for work performed—from transformational leadership, which seeks to appeal to followers' "better nature" and nudge them toward higher and shared purposes.

While there is a tendency for transactional leaders and followers to focus on immediate self-interest, transformational "leaders and followers raise one another to higher levels of morality and motivation" (Burns, 1978, p. 20). Transformational leaders are visionaries who appeal to values in an effort to present the big picture to their followers. Although they don't neglect individual goals, they recognize and emphasize a higher purpose, such as the purpose of an organization or a cause.

This model of leadership is of particular interest in this effort. We must first be transformed by the renewing of our minds before we can know the will of God for our lives (Romans 12:2). You will be more effective as a transformational leader when you've experienced transformation yourself.

While several other theories exist, the ones considered in this chapter represent much of the effort to develop a theory of leadership. Though no single model is foolproof, each represents an important perspective.

Notably, the different models aren't mutually exclusive. Leaders may need to oscillate between task and relationship orientations depending on the situation. They may need to combine team-based and transformational approaches depending on their purpose.

Now that we're done with theories, let's look into the attractive faces of leadership.

References

Barnes, L. B., and Kriger, M. F. (1986). The hidden side of organizational leadership. *Sloan Management Review*, 27, 15-25.

Burns, J. M. (1978). *Leadership.* New York: HarperCollins.

Coleman, J. (1999). *History of Political Thought.* MA: Blackwell Publishing.

George, S. (1961). *History of Political Theory.* London: H.R. and Winston, Inc.

Hershey, P., and Blanchard, K. H. (1977). *The Management of Organizational Behavior.* Upper Saddle River NJ: Prentice Hall.

House, R. J., and Mitchell, T. R. (1974). Path-goal theory of leadership. *Contemporary Business,* 3, Fall, 81-98.

Machiavelli, N. (1984). *The Prince.* New York: Bantam Classics.

Rost, J. C. (1991). *Leadership for the Twenty-first Century.* New York: Praeger.

CHAPTER 14

Faces of Leadership

Leadership is treasure! It is the key to unlocking and realizing your full potential. It is the means by which you identify, develop, organize, and invest your talent to reap the desired results. And it is the glue that holds the five aspects of *The Star Principle* together.

Leadership comprises several dimensions, each of which is relevant and often indispensable in your journey toward becoming all you were created to be.

Let's look at each of these dimensions to see how they apply to us.

Leadership is having, pursuing, and espousing a vision of a better future.

A vision is a picture or dream of the future that inspires and motivates us to act. The stronger the vision, the more it stimulates our mind, engages our body, and causes us to enlist people of like mind in bringing it to fruition. It's the means through which God's plan for our lives is revealed to us. That is why people fail without it (Proverbs 29:18).

Believers can receive visions directly or indirectly from God. A direct vision is when God speaks to a person audibly (as when He spoke to Moses), when He sends an angel (as in Zacharias' case), when He speaks in a trance or dream (as He did to Peter and Phillip), or when He speaks through His Spirit in us.

In biblical epochs, especially the Old Testament, God often spoke audibly and through angels and dreams because He needed to complete the work of redemption for humankind. That work, which commenced with God's covenant with Abraham, culminated in the death and resurrection of the Lord Jesus Christ. Today, everything we need to know about the ways of God is contained in the Bible. Although He reserves the right to speak to us in any manner, it is no longer necessary for Him to speak audibly or send angels.

However, God does still speak directly to our hearts. The Bible states that those "who are led by the Spirit of God are sons of God" (Romans 8:14 NIV). Being led by the Spirit implies the ability to hear from Him. First Corinthians 2:10 tells us that the Spirit knows the mind of God and reveals it to us. It is therefore perfectly appropriate to pray that God would reveal His will for you through His indwelling Spirit.

In a direct vision, God gives a clear and specific vision of the future. Abraham received a vision that he would be the father of nations and that his progeny would be as numerous as the stars. Noah was told to warn humanity of an impending flood. Peter received a specific vision to take the gospel to Macedonia. Paul saw a vision that transformed him from a persecutor of believers to a proponent of the faith.

Attempting to refine a direct vision is often an exercise in disobedience. It is tantamount to questioning God's authority. He expects immediate and complete obedience.

Indirect vision, which is more common in our generation, results from a process of *visioning* or *dreaming*. Visioning is what happens when we engage our talents, skills, and experiences in the thought process to formulate and refine an idea of a better future. We may call the product of this process an epiphany, a eureka moment, or sometimes a silly idea! The ideas constitute the dream of what we want to do with our lives, where we want to be when we retire, how we want to be remembered, or how we want to impact other people. They are, in essence, the road maps of our lives.

The things we do, places we go, and people we allow into our lives impact the visioning process. The thoughts your mind will generate and process in a clubhouse are different from the ones it will produce in the house of God. Likewise, counsel and guidance from your unsaved friends will yield different results from the advice you might receive from a man or woman of God, one of your Christian brothers and sisters.

When Samson started to mingle with Philistine women, he started to drift from his calling and dream about spending his life with them. Putting himself in the wrong environment cost him his life (Judges 16:4-30).

On the other hand, when Nebuchadnezzar, a worldly king, surrounded himself with God-fearing men, he began to see things he had never seen before and to develop a different worldview. He was so positively impacted by the godly people around him that he made a decree to defend the name of the almighty God (Daniel 3:29).

The gifts God has put in you are provisions for your vision. When you speak of having a natural flair for something, you are saying you have discovered your gift. As you refine it, you should dream of how you can maximize it. Try not to limit your dreaming. Allow the Spirit to guide you as your thoughts soar.

Sometimes people may not recognize their potential on their own. Good leaders can help pinpoint their natural strengths as well as their possibilities, and provide the encouragement and mentorship to enable them to dream. The calling of Peter, Andrew, John, and James is a prime example (Matthew 5:18-22). They didn't realize they could be great preachers and teachers and soul winners until Christ showed them how.

If we are walking by faith, the visions we conceive will be given to us by God. Our thoughts and resulting actions are inspired and guided by Him. Everything we engage in or that comes our way will be in accordance with His purpose for our lives.

God has planned for and expects us to dream. In Joel 2:28, He speaks of old men dreaming dreams and young men seeing visions after He has poured out His Spirit. His Spirit is already poured out, and we don't always have to be asleep to dream dreams or see visions. Through the enablement of the Holy Spirit, you can conceive things that are yet to come; that is, God's purpose for your life.

As a child of God, claim His promises. Dream! Don't worry about the specifics. As you seek Him in prayer and in the Word, ideas of your desired future will begin to spring up in your heart. They may seem lofty or farfetched or outright foreign. Don't discard them. Instead, follow the Lord's instruction: "Write the vision and make it plain on tablets, that he may run who reads it" (Habakkuk 2:2). Not only did Habakkuk have to write the vision, he was to refine it to the point that it would motivate the reader to act!

The difference between the multitude of fleeting ideas that cross your mind daily and the vision that will transform your life is that you pause to capture, in writing, the ideas you feel the Lord has placed in your heart concerning your future. It may take a lot of thinking and plenty of scrap paper, but your future is well worth the effort. If you're walking in complete obedience and constantly seeking the mind of God, you won't miss His impartation. Missteps, false positives, and counterfeit visions among believers are reflections of their degree of trust in the Lord. Believers who excel in a certain area of their lives, an area where they don't have difficulty trusting God, commonly stumble in other areas, where God is alienated.

Hardships can threaten a vision. However, they can refine you and prepare you to achieve your vision. God notes in Isaiah 48:10 that He refines us in the "furnace of adversity" (NRSV). A furnace suggests an engulfment of every part of your being. Needless to say, this can be an excruciating experience. However, God's furnace serves a good purpose: it burns off the sin nature—jagged edges of personality, character malignancy, hot temper, lust, doubt, fear, anger, etc.—to reveal the real you. Through it all, you must keep your vision in sight, as it's the only thing that will keep you focused.

A pastor friend shared the story of a general who led his army by sea to battle in a foreign country. On the way, some of his soldiers started to have doubts because of the distance and the fact that they had little information about the enemy. But the general had a vision: he was going to win the battle and return home within a predefined time frame. After they reached their destination, he burned the ships, their only mode of transportation and escape. They were either going to win the battle or die trying. That was the degree of his conviction. As the story goes, they won the battle and returned home in record time. If we can muster faith that's anywhere near the general's, there's no God-given vision that we won't fully achieve.

A vision is typically at odds with your present state of being. For instance, you may be a mailroom clerk today and dream of owning your own company in, say, five years. Since a dream is a personal experience, others may ridicule you if you share your vision in its infancy. They could come to the conclusion, by looking at your present condition, that you don't stand a chance. But a vision is not about the past or the present. It's about tomorrow. You don't need to have every provision for your vision before you can dream. God will supply all that you need to achieve it.

Here are three tests you can use to determine if your vision is in line with the will of God for your life. These tests aren't mutually exclusive; all three must align in validating any vision.

a. *Your vision must be in agreement with the Bible, which is the revealed Word of God.* God will not call you to found an abortion clinic or direct you to champion the legitimization of gay marriage. We are to prove everything to ensure it is the perfect will of God (Romans 12:2; 1 Thessalonians 5:21). This means asking several pointed questions as to the purpose of a vision before we embrace it to ensure it doesn't contradict Scripture.

The specifics of your vision shouldn't contradict God's Word either. Say God has purposed for you to be an investor. By pursuing this goal, you will be making a profit for yourself and your clients. However, if your plan is to make a profit by investing in pornographic videos and literature, that is not of God.

b. *Your vision must add value to someone else's life.* If your motivation is selfish or harmful to others, God is not in it. Luke's gospel tells the story of a farmer who had a superabundant harvest. Instead of seeking direction on how to manage the surplus, he dreamt only of eating, drinking, and being merry. As a result of his self-centeredness, he didn't live to enjoy any of the harvest (Luke 12:13-21).

Christ warned about false teachers and prophets (Matthew 24:24) who present themselves as channels of blessings and spiritual help. Their teachings are insidious, often leading thousands of people astray.

c. *You should be at peace with your vision.* If your vision is God's will for your life, there will be peace in your heart as you perform it. The Bible states that "God is not the author of confusion, but of peace" (1 Corinthians 14:33 KJV). He won't ask you to pursue anything that will lead to constant worry and heartache. Even with difficult assignments, peace and joy will fill your heart. In prison, Paul and Silas were joyful. They prayed and sang so earnestly that God shook apart the prison doors. They knew they were operating in obedience, and nothing—not even prison gates—could steal their peace.

Even in death, God's peace will guard your heart. As Christ hung on the cross with bruises all over His body, He prayed for the people who had caused Him so much pain. Stephen had unflappable peace as his accusers sought to kill him. As the crowd came close to stoning him, his mind was so focused on Christ he received a revelation of Him sitting at the right hand of the Father. Even as they cast the stones, he pleaded with God to forgive them (Acts 7:54-60).

The Bible declares in Isaiah 26:3 that God will keep your heart in perfect peace if you trust in Him. Thus, if your peace is perturbed, check your thoughts and actions. It might be that the indwelling Spirit of God is tugging at your heart, trying to get your attention before it's too late.

VISION ALIGNMENT TEST

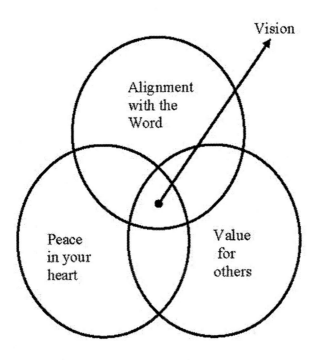

Remember, your vision must pass all three of these tests. For example, your vision may indeed bring value to others (test #2). But if you use value as the only measure, you may end up expending your energy doing someone else's work, only to realize midstream that your portion is waiting for you elsewhere. Many people feel as though they have fallen behind in their life's vision for this very reason.

You may wonder why your needs, wants, and desires are not at the center of your vision. The primary purpose for your vision is to please God. (See John 8:29; 4:34; Mark 3:35.) He has a plan for all of humanity, and He needs you to accomplish it. If you do not put Him first, you cannot enjoy divine guidance and empowerment.

Once you give God priority in your life, you will discover that pleasing Him is a two-part process: a walk of obedience and service to others. (See Matthew 28:19; 5:13-15; Mark 9:35; Romans 15:2-3; Ephesians 6:7.) Think about what He is asking you to do. How can your intellectual ability, technical skill, business acumen, wealth, and other resources He has given you benefit Him? He is an all-sufficient God and truly doesn't need anything from us. However, because He loves us so much, He requires us to spread His love and goodness throughout the world. We praise, worship, and serve Him because He is our Maker and the Lord of all creation, and because of His enduring love for us.

Our blessings and prosperity (and all the wonderful things we would like to have and enjoy), flow from a life of obedience and service. As you walk by faith and serve according to the abilities God has given you, He will bless and prosper you. He will supply your needs and exceed your expectations (Philippians 4:19; Ephesians 3:20).

You don't have to be a member of clergy to live a life of service. Irrespective of your occupation, as long as it doesn't contradict God's Word, and you believe it's what He has purposed for you, give it your best effort, as if you were working directly for the Lord (Ecclesiastics 9:10). You will shine like the star that you are, be an example to others, and bring blessings into your life.

Leadership is love.

Pursuing and achieving a vision requires more than a passing commitment. It takes complete and passionate devotion. You should love your vision so much you're willing and ready to do whatever it takes, within scriptural limits, to achieve it. You will burn the midnight oil, risk your life savings, venture into new territories. That is the spirit of a leader.

God loves us so much that after the fall in the garden, He found a way to reenact our relationship with Him. Christ, our model leader, loves us so dearly He gave His life for us. In his words, "Greater love has no man than this, that he lay down his life for his friends" (John 15:13 NIV). Thankfully, very rarely are we called upon to literally die on behalf of others. However, in those occasions where a sacrifice is called for, keep in mind that your sacrifices aren't in vain. In his path to stardom, Joseph encountered an adulterous woman and her actions landed him in jail. Little did he know that God was positioning him for his destiny.

No one is beyond giving or receiving love. We have to know what love is before we can give or receive it. Paul describes love as the greatest of virtues. It is a genuine, pure, open expression of affection and caring for someone or something. (See 2 Corinthians 13:1-13 for a detailed description.)

People who are unable to give or receive love are in critical need of God in their lives. God is love, and anyone who has a true encounter with Him is able to love and be loved.

Love enables us to accept our purpose. It supplies motivation for unwavering obedience to the Father. There couldn't have been a greater reason for Christ to die on our behalf. You may be comfortable where you are, just as Moses was with his in-laws after he fled Egypt. But God might be calling you to a different place. Love will enable you to leave your comfort zone and reach for the higher calling.

Love is the most powerful way to keep a dream alive. Since it never fails or gives up, love will help you stay focused in trying times. Love kept Christ from quitting in the garden of Gethsemane, and it enabled him to endure relentless beatings on the way to Calvary. Regardless of the circumstances you face, if you allow God's love to fill your heart, you will achieve your God-given purpose.

Jesus commands us to love our enemies (Matthew 5:44; Luke 6:27). This is difficult to accomplish if the love of God isn't given prominence in our hearts. Love is one virtue the enemy cannot overcome. There's no antidote for it. It's stronger than hate. If you learn to love your enemy, that enemy will soon be won over, defeated, softened, or driven off.

In many workplaces, *love* is a politically incorrect term. This is due in part to the existence of several versions and perversions of it. Infatuation, lust, and inordinate desire are some familiar variations. Few business leaders want to be remembered for any of these connotations. But love is the best gift anyone can give. Romans 13:8 counsels us to owe no one anything "except to love one another" (AMP). It's a great way to get the right result.

In trying to get Peter to feed His sheep, Jesus repeatedly asked him if he loved Him. By asking the same question three times, Christ was teaching us that true love will get us to do the right thing, all the time. As the Messiah, He could have threatened Peter with fire and brimstone. But He needed Peter to serve from the heart in His absence.

God loved us first. First John 4:10 puts it in perspective: "Herein is love, not that we loved God, but that he loved us, and sent his Son to be the propitiation for our sins" (KJV). Verse 19 concludes that "we love him, because he first loved us." He loves us so much, Paul declared, that nothing can separate us from Him (Romans 8:35-39).

Leadership is selfless service.

How often do we see people who parade themselves as icons of selflessness and altruism suddenly morph into insatiable piranhas after they move into a corner office? Such people only wear emblems of selflessness. They are self-serving leaders looking to beguile and exploit the innocent and unsuspecting.

Leadership at any level is a call to serve. It requires a prioritization that puts God first, others next, and self last. Contrary to what society has taught us, the "me first" philosophy is not a godly attitude. Jesus commanded us to put the kingdom of God first (Matthew 6:33).

God cannot be subject to any other authority. If we want Him in our lives, we must be willing to give up control. His intent isn't to render us powerless. He isn't interested in dictating our every decision. His goal is to lead us in the path of righteousness so we can achieve our purpose.

The Scriptures provide several examples of men and women who put God first. Abraham had to pack up and move to a different country because God wanted to raise a people for Himself. Moses left his family to confront Pharaoh because God wanted to liberate Israel. Joshua was given the task of leading them into the Promised Land. Esther was chosen to preserve the lives of her people. Mary was selected to birth the Messiah. Peter, Andrew, James, and John had to give up fishing to follow Christ. These individuals would have failed in realizing their full potential if they didn't put God first.

We learn in Philippians 2:3 that we should esteem others better than ourselves. We should radiate humility in our dealings with others. Christ added another critical nugget by teaching His disciples that serving is the road to greatness. He taught them to replace self-serving tendencies with a servant-leader attitude. By putting others first, you are exercising faith and giving God an opportunity to work on your behalf. And you will be greatly rewarded (Matthew 10:42; Proverbs 11:18).

Self-serving leaders have been around for ages. Avoid them! They offer a nightmare, not a dream. Isaiah lamented that such people are "greedy dogs which can never have enough, and they are shepherds that cannot understand: they all look to their own way, every one for his gain, from his quarter" (Isaiah 56:11 KJV).

An act doesn't need to be heroic to be selfless. Doing things for the right reason, giving your best effort, lending a helping hand as needed, sharing the spotlight with others, and making reasonable sacrifices to sustain a vision are all relevant to building a selfless reputation. They will all count toward achieving your full potential.

Leadership is being able to act decisively.

People who suffer from abulia—that is, the lack of ability to make decisions—have a difficult time as leaders. Leaders drive a vision by their decisions and actions. If they act too slowly, they may lose momentum and the vision may fizzle out. If they act too quickly, they may make costly mistakes. It therefore behooves them to learn to make informed, timely decisions.

A decision implies taking a stand on your convictions, on what you believe to be right. The future, as you visualize it, is a personal experience. If you don't believe in it enough to take action, it will probably never come to fruition. People will respond to faith in your vision as demonstrated by your decision and resulting action.

A doubtful person is in danger of being unable to achieve his or her full potential. The Bible describes such a person as unstable in all his ways (James 1:8). Jesus expressed disdain for such instability. He said He preferred that people be either hot or cold (have a clear position). Those who are neither here nor there will receive the same judgment as those who are cold toward the things of God (Revelation 3:15-16). The double-minded person must work hard to purify his heart. He must learn to make abiding decisions (James 4:8). And he must mix faith with the Word so he can act on his vision (Hebrews 4:2).

People who have difficulty with decision-making also have a hard time taking responsibility for their actions. Like the third servant in the parable of the talents, they expend their energy crafting excuses instead of making right decisions. When excuses replace important decisions, they result in a diminishing modification to our future. Some would argue that excuses can get us out of sticky situations. However, if we make right decisions in the first place, we won't find ourselves in sticky situations.

Sometimes people draw back from making decisions because they're afraid of being wrong. But God expects us to make decisions by considering the information available to us in light of His Word and taking the best course of action. In our fast-paced environment, you may not have all the information you *want* to comfortably make a decision. But God will always supply what you *need* according to His Word (Philippians 4:19). He is all knowing and ever present with you. He already knows what is right. Make a habit of committing every decision to Him, even when you think you're right. That demonstrates your total reliance on Him.

Leadership is finding opportunity in adversity.

Christ warned that adversity is bound to come (John 16:33). It comes as sickness, pain, bereavement, unemployment, divorce, slander, oppression, deprivation, and other forms. It has no regard for personality, class, or any other social distinction.

Adversity comes for four major reasons:

a. To glorify God. Sometimes difficulties arise so we can experience the miraculous power of God and so that others may see, believe, and glorify God. When Jesus was told his friend Lazarus was sick, He responded that the "sickness will not end in death." He added that it was "for God's glory so that God's Son may be glorified through it" (John 11:4 NIV). Instead of fretting or complaining, we should seek opportunities to glorify God through our difficult situations.

On another occasion, Jesus and His disciples saw a man who had been blind from birth. The disciples asked if the man's or his parents' sin had caused the blindness. Jesus answered that neither the man nor his parents had sinned. He noted that his condition was to allow for the manifestation of the power of God (John 9:1-3).

Every miracle is a testimony, and the more testimonies we have, the stronger our faith will be. If God healed you of a terminal disease, you would be able to speak confidently about His healing power. Better yet, you might become a vessel through which He would heal other people suffering from diverse illnesses. Ultimately, others would overcome their adversities based on your testimony.

b. Adversity prepares us for our desired future. There is a lesson in every hardship, and it is our responsibility to discover and learn it. Indeed, the sooner we realize what God is trying to teach us, the quicker we can get out of the difficult situation. Time and again, the children of Israel learned the hard way. God worked hard to build up their faith, but they ignored Him and reveled in doubt. Their actions added forty years to their suffering.

The prodigal son came to his senses after he squandered his portion of the family wealth. He needed to eschew greed and learn humility. Had anyone tried to teach him humility, he probably would have balked. But when humiliation and hunger set in, they were more than enough to bend his will.

Paul summarizes the didactic value of adversity in this passage of Scripture: "We also rejoice in our sufferings, because we know that suffering produces perseverance; perseverance, character; and character, hope. And hope does not disappoint" (Romans 5:3-5 NIV). We are able to rejoice because we know adversity will leave us better than we were.

c. Adversity is one way God gets the attention of His children. Once more, Jonah comes to mind. He refused to carry out an assignment God gave him until he experienced pain. After the death of the child that resulted from the adulterous relationship between David and Bathsheba, he no longer took adultery lightly.

Hebrews 12:11 teaches us the value of discipline: "No discipline seems pleasant at the time, but painful. Later on, however, it produces a harvest of righteousness and peace for those who have been trained by it" (NIV).

God disciplines us out of love so we may be restored to the path of righteousness (Hebrews 12:6).

d. A sinful or disobedient lifestyle can lead to many adversities. Since we're responsible for what we know, God expects us to act on the basis of our knowledge. If, after we have tasted the truth, we reject it, the Bible warns that there's no more remedy for sin. A life of rebellion leads to suffering and destruction (Hebrews 10:26). For this reason Eli and his family were destroyed. (See 1 Samuel 3:12-14.)

Leaders don't allow adversity to detract from their vision. Instead of succumbing, they seek out the lesson or opportunity in it.

In 1981, a tornado struck one of the then Sound of Music stores in Roseville, Minnesota. Instead of closing down the store or relocating, the company responded with a "Tornado Sale." The sale was so successful it held a second tornado sale in 1982. By 1983, it introduced superstores and changed its name to Best Buy Co., Inc.

The amazing turnaround would have gone unrealized had Richard Schulze given up on his vision for the Roseville location. (Visit http://www.bestbuy.com for a chronological history of Best Buy Co., Inc.)

Leadership is bringing out the best in others.

One of the most delightful roles of a leader is to release the potential in others. A good leader can see beyond the veneer of rawness and inexperience to unlock the star within. Jesus exemplified this dimension of leadership when He chose His disciples. Peter, his brother Andrew, and James and John, sons of Zebedee, were fishermen when Jesus met them. He needed men who would be His ambassadors on earth, men who would articulate and present the gospel to the entire world. Religious leaders, intellectuals, and powerful political leaders could have been first on His list. But He saw all the talent He needed in these individuals. If they were proficient in catching fish, He could teach them proficiency in converting people.

Jesus and Matthew had very little in common when they met. Matthew was a tax collector. He took money from his own people to give to the authorities in Rome, so not much love was lost between him and his people. However, Jesus stopped by Matthew's collection post and extended an invitation to him. When the Pharisees later saw them dining together, they were shocked and wondered why the Messiah would dine with a tax collector. From their perspective, they didn't belong together. But to the Savior, Matthew had what it took to get the job done.

To be of significant help, a leader has to spend time getting to know and understand his or her followers. Based on this knowledge, teaching, coaching, guidance, and correction can occur. Patience is often necessary throughout these steps. Jesus spent a great deal of time with His disciples. He gave them knowledge that He withheld from the general public. Furthermore, He fielded their questions and taught them how to lead a victorious life.

Motivation or encouragement from a leader holds significant value. Breakthroughs result from it. Great leaders motivate their followers in both word and action. They focus on and reinforce right behavior. After making excuses, Moses decided to confront Pharaoh because the Lord proved to him in word and deed that He would be with him (Genesis 3:9-22; 4:1-17). Joshua was fired up after a few words of encouragement from God (Joshua 1:2-9). Jeremiah had trouble starting his ministry because he felt he was a child. Again, a word of encouragement from the Father was all it took to get him going (Jeremiah 1:5-8).

Since your vision is tied to other people, it is in your best interest to help them reach their full potential. If you do, your own vision will be that much more successful. In teaching, guiding, and empowering His disciples, Jesus ensured that the gospel would reach you and me.

Leadership is being a conscientious follower.

Christ has called us to be like Him (Matthew 16:24; 4:19; 8:22). Your degree of success in becoming like Him is proportionate to how closely, carefully, and faithfully you follow His steps. It is not enough to believe in His teaching, have a general idea of the gospel, or be a nominal Christian. The operative word that Peter identified in 1 Peter 2:21 is "steps." It means doing what Christ would do in any situation you find yourself. Like the psalmist, we should always pray for the Lord to order our steps (Psalm 119:133).

A conscientious follower is attentive to every move of his leader. Being alert at all times is a surefire way to learn from rare occurrences or one-time events. Elisha exemplified this level of consciousness. His master, Elijah, knew the Lord was ready to take him and wanted to be alone for his departure. He embarked on a journey and entreated Elisha not to follow him. Being an attentive follower, Elisha knew Elijah was about to leave him for good and didn't want to miss the moment.

When Elisha continued to follow him after several pleas to

cease, Elijah gave him an opportunity to ask whatever he wanted. He asked for a double portion of the spirit that was on his master. The only way his request would be granted was if he saw Elijah being taken up. Though he didn't know the time or place the ascension would occur, he was careful not to miss the moment. Consequently, he got the blessing he asked for (2 Kings 1-12).

Although they were mostly diligent in following Christ, Peter, James, and John disappointed Him at a time of difficulty. Of all His disciples, He picked the three of them to pray with Him in Gethsemane. As He poured out His sorrowful heart to the Father, these disciples fell asleep. Twice He came by to wake them up so they could support Him in prayer but sleep got the best of them. It appeared they did not appreciate the agony their master was going through. Jesus thought He could count on them at a time when death stared Him in the face, but they let Him down (Matthew 26:36-46).

Can your leader count on you when the going gets tough? Remember, those behind you are paying close attention to your actions. They will likely follow your example.

Leaders who make good followers are excellent listeners. They pay attention to the nuances of the signals and messages their leaders evince. When Jesus told Peter he would deny Him trice, Peter wasn't listening. His Savior was speaking prophetically, and instead of taking in the word and asking for help, he argued with Him. The end result was that he denied Christ three times. He cried afterward, but the tears should have been shed when he got the message (Mark 14:27-31; 14:66-72).

To be clear, there's a place and time to challenge your leader. Indeed, it takes a conscientious follower to know when a leader is going astray. Naaman's servant confronted Naaman when he declined to follow Elisha's instruction to bathe in the River Jordan. The servant knew the prophet's instruction was in his master's best interest. He summoned the courage to say so. Following his advise, Naaman bathed in the River and was cured of leprosy (2 Kings 5:9-14).

Conscientious followers know when to pick up the pace and when to stop. They know when to ask a question of their leader and when to seek out their own answer. They know how to leave markers and footprints so those behind them can learn from their experiences.

Leadership is standing in the gap for followers.

Leadership involves taking a risk for the well-being of followers. A good leader believes in his cause and the dedication of those behind him enough to take responsibility for their actions or do battle on their behalf.

Although Lot wasn't as respectful as he could have been to his uncle, Abraham went to bat for him when the Lord revealed that He was going to destroy Sodom and Gomorrah. Lot lived in Sodom and would have died along with the other residents had Abraham not interceded persistently for him and his family (Genesis 18:16-33).

Moses went as far as offering his life for rebellious Israel. His followers were so stubborn, faithless, and ungrateful that God wanted to destroy them and raise a new people for Himself (Deuteronomy 9:14). A self-serving leader would have consented to the offer. But Moses believed in the shared vision of liberation for his people to the point that he asked God to strike his name from the book of life instead of destroying them. His action reflects the spirit of a true leader (Exodus 32:32).

Esther also balked tradition and put her life on the line for her people. She needed an invitation to enter the inner court of the king to speak with him, but time wasn't on her side. So she fasted and prayed and arranged the meeting with the king. The outcome of the meeting couldn't have been more favorable (Esther 4:1-17; 5:1-14; 6:1-14).

Good leaders watch over their followers. As Peter's spiritual leader, Christ foresaw that the devil wanted to do a number on Peter. He prayed for him before He revealed the knowledge. Since it was a personal matter, He shared the information when He was alone with Peter (Luke 22:31-32).

If you find this dimension of leadership challenging to embrace, remember that Christ stood in the gap for all of us. With His blood, He wrote off our debt of sin so we can get a fresh start. Why wouldn't you tolerate a relatively small discomfort to give your fellow human being a break?

FACES OF LEADERSHIP: PRACTICE AID

1. Having, pursuing, and espousing a vision of a better future	2.
3.	4.
5.	6.
7.	8.

Make a copy of this chart or print from www.starprinciple.com. Pick one of the eight faces of leadership you would like to develop or incorporate into your style. I encourage you to start with *having, pursuing, and espousing a vision of a better future.* Write it in one of the boxes and post it where it's visible to you. Move on to the next face only after it's second nature.

Star Leadership®, a Christian consulting organization that focuses on enabling individuals and teams to develop their leadership skills and achieve their *full* potential, offers seminars that will assist you in releasing your leadership potential. Visit the above Web site for a list of current offerings.

CHAPTER 15

Readiness Assessment

Much of existing literature examines leadership only as a social concept. The spectrum often ranges from family to global leadership. Researchers focus on how family, business, political, and religious leaders enable the entities they lead to achieve success.

What's often ignored is the process of preparation and development that enables an individual to release his leadership potential. An individual who is unable to effectively lead himself cannot successfully lead others.

Imagine having a person who is uncertain about his or her vision trying to influence and guide others toward achieving that vision; or a person who has run from every major personal responsibility attempting to act decisively on behalf of others; or a person who is used to surrendering to personal challenges trying to lead others beyond adversity; or a person who doesn't know what he excels at the most trying to bring out the best in others; or a self hater trying to be a caring and loving role model; or a self-serving person promising selfless service. Christ said about such individuals, "You hypocrite, first take the plank out of your own eye, and then you will see clearly to remove the speck from your brother's eye" (Matthew 7:5 NIV). Sadly, given the level of poverty, suffering, and mediocrity among

God's children, it's likely that many of the people with whom we're aligned in pursuing our destinies have difficulty leading themselves.

How does a person transform from being unprepared to a knowledgeable and successful leader positioned to achieve his God-given purpose? How can a person successfully discover more about himself, seek a relationship with his Maker, learn discipline, envision and pursue a brighter future, and achieve and sustain that future? And is that process repeatable?

Self-leadership enables you to identify and implement the steps needed to achieve your intended purpose through the focus and discipline it provides. Put differently, by developing strong self-leadership skills, you can achieve your full potential.

Fundamentally, self-leadership asserts that every person is created to be a leader. Everyone needs a vision and an understanding of how it can be achieved. The will to achieve the vision must come from within. As much as some people would like to thrust their lives on others, there's a divinely appointed purpose for which each person is accountable. As Paul put it, "each of us will give an account of himself to God" (Romans 14:12 NIV).

Effectively leading oneself is a prerequisite for leading others. Self-leadership allows the individual to focus on self-preparation. It enables him or her to seek an understanding of self relative to faith, purpose, character, and readiness to achieve the desired future. The individual must conduct a realistic self-assessment in order to determine what steps should be taken to facilitate movement in the right direction.

Ultimately, self-leadership is about making choices. Those choices will determine whether we achieve our full potential. If, for instance, we lack the discipline or will to follow through with our choices, we run the risk of missing out on God's plan for our lives. We cannot achieve our full potential, let alone lead others to achieve theirs, with poor self-leadership skills. Attaining all that God has prepared for us requires unwavering faith, commitment, and conviction.

Leading self and others.

For our purposes, *leadership* is the ability to mobilize self, and then others, to achieve a common vision.

Effectively leading self will naturally pull you toward people who share your vision. This happens as you obey the Lord's command to clearly articulate your vision, and as you follow Paul's counsel to be up front about your moral values (Philippians 4:5). Your prospect of being an effective leader is greatly enhanced by the experience you gain when you apply leadership principles to yourself.

As a leader, it behooves you to teach your followers the wisdom of self-leadership. Having everyone on the same page will strengthen the team's vision. You won't have to do as much selling or persuading if people understand that their destinies are tied to the vision. Each person will focus on his or her portion of the effort required to achieve the vision. The drive to achieve their full potential will create a level of teamwork and synergy that can only result in exponential success. Eventually, what will emerge is what Paul describes as a body with many parts, with each part functioning in coordination with the rest of the body to maximize efficiency and produce optimal results (1 Corinthians 12:12).

This was the experience of the early church. The favor and supernatural power they experienced came mainly because they were of one accord (Acts 5:12-16). This experience is being reenacted by a few organizations throughout the world. If you're willing to take the right steps, you will have the same results.

Where are you today?

Each of us is at a different place in the effort to achieve the future God has designed for us. Instead of bemoaning what has been, or what is, let us begin a concerted effort to shape what is yet to be. As George Elliot (1819-1880) once said, "It's never too late to be what you might have been" (March 25, 2005. <www.writersmugs/quote/George_Eliot/141.html>).

The Bible declares that *now* is the accepted time; today is the day of salvation (2 Corinthians 6:2). What you do now will determine what you become tomorrow. To neglect this call, or put it off to another day, is to ignore what is rightfully yours. Remember, tomorrow is not guaranteed to any of us.

If you hesitate to take action for personal reasons, consider that you might be sitting on someone else's blessing. You could be holding back the blessing of an entire family, or even a nation. The individual or group might be praying day and night for God's move, and God might be counting on you to meet their needs. If you don't respond, God will still take care of His own. However, you will have to account for your inaction or disobedience.

Taking charge of your life will not only brighten your future, it will increase your potential of being a beacon of light to those around you.

Self-leadership Assessment.

The critical next step is a careful and honest examination of your life to determine what you need to do to experience the fullness of what God has purposed for you. The Self-Leadership Assessment® (SLA) overleaf is designed to help you determine where you stand relative to self-leadership. For it to yield the desired result, you must take responsibility for the totality of your experiences and actions. Having an honest aspiration to become all that you've been created to be will help you keep an open mind and take whatever steps may be necessary to correct deficiencies.

SELF-LEADERSHIP ASSESSMENT® Please check a box for each of the following statements. A = True;B =Somewhat True;C =Not Sure;D=Not True		Points
Section One: Self-Discovery		
I have accepted Christ as my Lord and Savior.	[A] [B] [C] [D]	
I believe God has a purpose for my life.	[A] [B] [C] [D]	
I am a star.	[A] [B] [C] [D]	
I understand my strengths and weaknesses.	[A] [B] [C] [D]	
I have confronted and overcome every personal weakness that I am aware of.	[A] [B] [C] [D]	
Total		
Section Two: Spiritual Development		
I believe unequivocally that the Bible is the Word of God.	[A] [B] [C] [D]	
I put God first in all my decisions.	[A] [B] [C] [D]	
I always make godly confessions over my life.	[A] [B] [C] [D]	
I am a product of my thoughts and actions.	[A] [B] [C] [D]	
I always act by faith.	[A] [B] [C] [D]	
Total		
Section Three: Character Development		
I will stand up for truth at any cost.	[A] [B] [C] [D]	
My moral values derive from the Word of God.	[A] [B] [C] [D]	
My actions always match my words.	[A] [B] [C] [D]	
I am always on time, always consistent, and always prepared.	[A] [B] [C] [D]	
I treat everyone justly and fairly.	[A] [B] [C] [D]	
Total		

Section Four: Resilience Development		
I am at a place in my faith walk where nothing/ no one can stop me from achieving my destiny.	[A] [B] [C] [D]	
I always depend on the Lord to fight my battles.	[A] [B] [C] [D]	
I am helping others to achieve their potential.	[A] [B] [C] [D]	
I always fulfill my vows and promises.	[A] [B] [C] [D]	
I believe sharing is critical to my prosperity.	[A] [B] [C] [D]	
Total		
Section Five: Self-Leadership		
I understand the essence of leadership in achieving my full potential.	[A] [B] [C] [D]	
I am an effective self-leader.	[A] [B] [C] [D]	
My vision aligns with God's will for my life.	[A] [B] [C] [D]	
I look for opportunity in every adversity.	[A] [B] [C] [D]	
The love of God fills my heart and flows through me to others.	[A] [B] [C] [D]	
Total		

This Self-Leadership Assessment has been reformatted to fit this page. You may print a copy of the original version at www.starprinciple.com.

*** It is important to read the entire book before completing this assessment. The questions are based on topics addressed in the book.*

Instructions for the Self-Leadership Assessment.

The SLA is divided into five sections, each one representing a dimension of *The Star Principle*. Each section is composed of five statements. There are four possible responses to each statement: True, Somewhat True, Not Sure, and Not True. Check one response per statement. It is important that you respond to all of the statements.

Each response has been assigned a number of points that will help you plot your results on a graph.

True	= 20 points
Somewhat True	= 10 points

Not Sure = 0 points
Not True = -20 (negative 20 points)

Add up your responses in the column titled "Points." If you check "True" on all the statements in a section, you will have a total of 100 points. You will have 50 points if you check "Somewhat True" and 0 points if you check "Not Sure." Your total will be -100 if you check "Not True" on all five statements in a section.

How to interpret your result.

Your responses will fall into one of three categories: Ready (500 points), Somewhat Ready (250 to 499 points), and Not Ready (0 to 249 points).

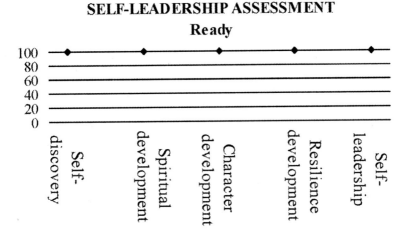

SELF-LEADERSHIP ASSESSMENT
Ready

Ready (500 points): Since the statements mainly reflect the irreducible level of self-leadership you must attain to achieve your full potential, you must score 100 points in every section to be in this category. Your chart should be an exact replica of the one above. You have been saved through faith in the Lord Jesus Christ. You've learned how to advance your faith and future by trusting, meditating on, confessing, and applying the Word of God.

You've cultivated a character that is beyond reproach. Your values line up with Scripture and you're not afraid to practice them.

People around you can testify to the beauty of Christ that radiates through your speech, action, behavior, and presence.

Irreproachability of character doesn't imply that you never make mistakes. But when you do, you take responsibility for your action and immediately take corrective measures.

Readiness indicates you've become adept at using spiritual principles to fight opposition and overcome obstacles. The enemy is afraid of you because he knows you never lose a battle. God's wall of protection surrounds you, favor goes ahead of you, and goodness and mercy follow you every day and everywhere.

Readiness denotes that you have, and are actively pursuing, a vision for your life. You believe this vision is in alignment with the will of God for you, and although there may not be a significant physical manifestation yet, the Word and the Spirit of God in you confirm that you're on the right path.

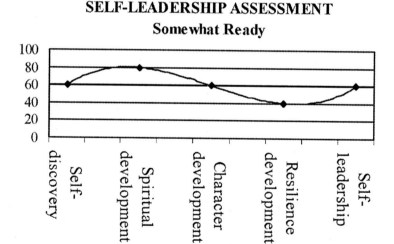

SELF-LEADERSHIP ASSESSMENT
Somewhat Ready

Somewhat Ready (250 to 499 points): You excel in some areas but have a few deficiencies. Your first step is to identify these deficiencies and recognize them as areas of opportunity for improvement.

The most important aspect of your readiness is salvation. If you're not absolutely sure you're saved, you won't reap the full benefit of *The Star Principle*. Far worse, you stand in danger of eternal condemnation.

To experience salvation *now*, ask the Lord Jesus Christ to come into your life to be your Lord and Savior. Believe in your heart that He died for your sins and God raised Him from the dead. Confess your sins before Him and ask for forgiveness. He will hear your prayer and come into your life. (See Romans 10:9-10; John 3:16; John 1:12.) Next, find a Bible-believing church where you will be taught the Word of God.

If you have opportunities for improvement in any other area, conduct a root-cause analysis to determine the origin of the problem. The weakness you've identified may be symptomatic of a more severe, underlying problem.

Begin your analysis by probing your life for clues. Ask yourself the following questions: What action did I take or not take that got me where I am? What behavior facilitated my drive in the wrong direction? Who or what else contributed to my getting here? How long have I been in this position? What can I do differently in the future? Who or what can facilitate my movement in the right direction?

The answers to the above questions will help you develop a Corrective Action Plan (CAP) to facilitate your desired improvement. Your CAP should include Specific, Measurable, Aligned, Realistic, and Time-bound (SMART) goals. *Alignment* means it agrees with the Word, *realistic* implies that it's achievable, and *time-bound* means it must be achieved within a defined period of time. Specificity is necessary to avoid confusion and to help you meet your goals in a timely manner. If the goal isn't measurable, you may not be able to tell when you've achieved it.

Prayer must be the first solution. It will enable all the other corrective steps to produce the right result.

Put your CAP in writing. This action validates that you're serious about it and helps you to recall what you've set out to change. Review it often to ensure that your actions are consistent with the plan.

Identify the steps you must take if you don't achieve your plan in the initial time limit, but avoid tweaking it often to accommodate lapses. It's better to get a realistic assessment and seek help as needed than to gloss over problems or force them to fit the plan.

Visit www.starprinciple.com for resources that will assist you as you create your plan. Free Christian mentoring is also available on the site.

Keep track of the steps you find useful in overcoming obstacles. You may need to adopt them into your lifestyle when the corrective plan expires.

CORRECTIVE ACTION PLAN
John Q

Opportunity Areas
1. Weak prayer life.
2. Poor time-management skill.

Goals
1. To pray twice daily, for a minimum of twenty minutes each time, between now and May 10.

2. To be on time to church, work, school, and any other place, event, or meeting between now and May 10.

3. To make a habit of goals #1 and #2 at the end of this corrective action process.

Action Steps
Prayer life:
(a) Commit plan to God in prayer.
(b) Set alarm clock to 5:30 AM, thirty minutes earlier than usual.
(c) Move Friday-night outing with friends from 6:00 to 6:30 PM.
(d) Use den as prayer room to minimize interruption.
(e) Consistently attend prayer gatherings at church.
(f) Share plan with family members and solicit their support and cooperation.

Time management:

(a) Commit plan to God in prayer.

(b) Identify my daily and weekly activities and organize them on my calendar.

(c) Carry the calendar with me at all times and update as necessary. Upgrade to a PDA by May 30.

(d) Where possible, build preparation and travel time into the calendar.

(e) Read a good time-management book by May 10.

(f) Share plan with family members and solicit their support and cooperation.

Next Steps

If plan is successful,

1. Celebrate success with family and friends.

2. Determine and permanently adopt useful CAP steps._

If prayer plan is unsuccessful,

1. Conduct another root-cause analysis.

2. Ask a family member or friend to join me.

3. Seek counsel from another Christian.

4. Repeat action steps a through e.

If time-management plan is unsuccessful,

1. Pray fervently for strength to achieve the plan.

2. Conduct another root-cause analysis.

3. Take a time-management class.

Creating an environment that's conducive to change should be on every action plan. It's nearly impossible to achieve lasting success without it. We operate in two environments, spiritual and physical, and we cannot afford to care for one and not the other.

Preparing your spiritual environment involves having a heart that's amenable to change. Even your best plans will fail if your heart isn't totally submitted to the Spirit of God. You can begin by asking, like the psalmist, for a clean and receptive heart (Psalm 51:10).

After your heart is transformed, don't leave it fallow. The Bible teaches that the enemy will populate it and your latter condition will be worse than the former (Matthew 12:43-45). Make determined efforts to fill your heart with the Word. In addition to self-study of the Scriptures, find Christian books, music, Web sites, and other resources that will increase your understanding, especially in your opportunity area.

If you have not done so already, find a true Bible-believing church where you will be taught the Word on a regular basis. The Bible counsels us not to ignore the gathering of the children of God (Hebrews 10:25). Earnestly pray and seek guidance as you search for a church home. Perhaps the worst thing that can happen at this point is to expose yourself to false doctrine.

Next, take steps in your physical environment to reinforce your spiritual resolve. If, for instance, you struggle with pornography, remove all magazines with nude or scantily clad women (including most dress catalogues) from your house, office, or places you frequent. Invest in software that prevents pornographic materials from popping up while surfing the Web. If your cable or satellite TV airs pornographic programs, either find a way to deactivate those channels or terminate the service altogether. Separate yourself from friends who derive pleasure from pornography.

The Bible advises us to flee temptation or any presence of evil (Psalm 34:14; 1 Corinthians 6:18; 10:14; 2 Timothy 2:22). Joseph, a God-fearing man, fled when Potiphar's wife tried to seduce him. He could have tried to talk her out of it. But he was wise enough to understand that there's a time to reason and a time to run! This advice takes on a higher level of significance when you're trying to change a habit. As the saying goes, old habits die hard.

Condoning vestiges of undesired habits as you try to turn a corner amounts to putting those habits on life support. Sooner or later you will give in to a craving and derail your plan. Even after the spiritual roots have been destroyed through the power of prayer and godly confession, quitting a habit requires a great deal of discipline. The good news is that God's grace is sufficient for you.

SELF-LEADERSHIP ASSESSMENT
Not Ready

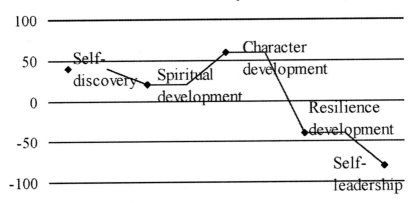

Not Ready (0 to 249 points): You're not yet in a position to receive God's purpose for your life. Now that you know where you stand, you can make a decision as to what steps you need to take to get ready.

The most important thing is to establish a relationship with God the Father through Jesus Christ, His Son. You do this by confessing and repenting of your sins and inviting Christ into your heart to be your Lord and Savior. Your sins will be wiped out and He will give you a new life (1 John 1:9; 2 Corinthians 5:17).

To help grow your spiritual life, find a good church where you will be taught the Word of God. Just as your body cannot function without food, your spiritual life will suffer without the Word.

As you begin to build your faith, form the habit of asking questions. Ask your spiritual leaders to teach you more about the concepts addressed in this book. I had the opportunity of listening to a series of sermons that was based on the manuscript for this book. The pastor applied his knowledge of the people and matters in his congregation to tailor a message around the key concepts of purpose, dream, and divine enablement.

After you have entered into a relationship with your Creator, consider the following resources for your plan:

a. Find a Christian mentor. This is someone you can approach for counsel and direction. He or she should be able to assist in preparing your action plan and be available as a resource as you implement the plan.

b. Take advantage of the free Open Mentoring® service provided by Star Leadership®. This Web-based service allows you to pose questions regarding your efforts to achieve your full potential to Christian experts. You can ask questions about faith, school, marriage, family, government, etc. The experts will address your concern and, if necessary, direct you to where you can find additional resources. All questions are addressed from a biblical perspective. Responses are posted on the Star Leadership® Web site: www.starprinciple.com. The intent is to enable all mentees with similar questions to benefit from the answers. You can elect not to have your name displayed with the response to your question. Visit the above Web site for details.

c. Consider attending a star seminar. Star Seminars® are offered by Star Leadership® and are designed to show you how you can become a better person, employee, supervisor, and leader. They provide training in self-leadership skills and teach you how to apply those skills in leading others and in building strong, high-performing teams. Ultimately, they help you understand how spiritual principles can enable you to achieve outstanding results in your secular employment. Visit www.starprinciple.com for a list of Star Seminars® that can assist you.

d. Seek professional help if you are confronting debt and financial problems, marital instability, depression, or other psychological problems, or if you struggle with drug, alcohol, sex, or any other form of addiction. Again, a list of resources is available on the above Web site.

Your CAP is going to require that you make sacrifices. In the process, you may lose some friends, and family members may reject you. But this isn't the time to succumb to the pressures. As Christ said, "No one, having put his hand to the plow, and looking back, is fit for the kingdom of God" (Luke 9:62). He added that it is better to enter into the kingdom of God with one eye and one arm than to subject the entire body to the flames of hellfire (Matthew 5:29-30).

Take comfort in the fact that you're not alone; God will be with you every step of the way. Your role is to make yourself available for His use; He will fulfill His purpose for your life (Psalm 138:8). Your fleeting difficulties will give way to a disproportionately greater reward (2 Corinthians 4:17). After you've been refined, God will make you perfect. He will establish, strengthen, and settle you (1 Peter 5:10). In the end, not only will you experience your intended future on earth, you will have the matchless honor of spending eternity with the Father, Son, and Holy Ghost!

Printed in the United States
31216LVS00005B/130-399